CITY FAMILIES

December 1980

Dear M & D,

I couldn't resist. The funny part is that even if they weren't grouped you could tell the pictures apart!

With Love, Abby

CITY FAMILIES

Chicago and London

BY ROSLYN BANISH

Pantheon Books

NEW YORK

All rights reserved under International and Pan-American
Copyright Conventions. Published in the United States by
Pantheon Books, a division of Random House, Inc., New
York, and simultaneously in Canada by Random House of
Canada Limited, Toronto.

Library of Congress Cataloging in Publication Data

Main entry under title:
City Families: Chicago and London.

Consists of interviews and accompanying photos of
80 families.
   1. Photography—Portraits. 2. Family—London.
3. Family—Chicago. I. Banish, Roslyn, 1942–
TR681.F28C57 779′.2 76-9981
ISBN 0-394-49906-9
ISBN 0-394-73236-7 pbk.

Manufactured in the United States of America
Design by Kenneth A. Miyamoto

FIRST EDITION

To PAE

ACKNOWLEDGMENTS

First and foremost, my thanks to all those families in London and Chicago, including the families that do not appear in the final selection, who were willing to be photographed and interviewed. This book depends on them.

My appreciation to those individuals and institutions who helped me recruit families, including the many people who asked their friends and neighbors on my behalf. To name a few:

In London:
Mrs. Goss, Abbot's Manor Toddlers Club
the staff of the Maternal and Child Health Clinic, Ebury Bridge Road
Dr. Robert Morris
Denise Dennehy

In Chicago:
Mary Crane Nursery School, Family and Day Care Center
St. Vincent De Paul Center
Lincoln Park Neighborhood Senior Center, Clark-Webster building
Mr. and Mrs. Fred Odanaka

Special thanks to the Arts Council of Great Britain for giving me a grant which made the initial photography possible, and in particular to Barry Lane at the Arts Council, who was the first to believe in my idea; to Nicholas Woolley, who showed me how to interview and who gave me the confidence to do so; to Carolyn Jennings and Rod Nordberg for their painstaking transcriptions of the taped interviews; to Doris Adelstein and Lee Haupt for their skills with the English language; to Tony Gibbons and Joel Snyder for assorted friendly advice; and to my other friends in London and Chicago who looked at and discussed with me the work in progress, whose judgment I respect.

My appreciation also to Sylvia Cooper and Nigel Earthy, Midland Group Gallery, Nottingham, for first exhibiting my London portraits, "Family Portraits from Pimlico," March 1974; to the following publications for first publishing some of the London portraits: *Laurels*, East Midlands Art Association, Loughborough, England, Spring 1974; *Creative Camera*, Coo Press, London, England, November 1974; *British Image*, Arts Council of Great Britain, London, England, 1975.

And finally, my thanks to editor Barbara Plumb and Amy Huntoon at Pantheon for their enthusiasm and for seeing the book through the various stages of production.

INTRODUCTION

The idea for this book started simply with the desire to photograph ordinary English people in their homes. I had been living in London for about three and a half years, and I had an outsider's curiosity about my "adopted" environment, including a fascination with the look of things—all the details of ordinary dress and furnishings— and the unavoidable comparisons with things back home. Beyond a curiosity about the inside of English homes, there existed a more complex interest in English family life. Many of my experiences confirmed the old cliché "an Englishman's home is his castle," and I wanted to get inside and to photograph both the Englishman and his castle. In terms of photography, I felt that would represent unexplored territory. I had not come across photographs of English people at home in everyday situations since seeing Bill Brandt's pictures of the 1930s.

I set out to photograph a cross-section of English families in their homes. I chose a neighborhood in central London in which many different classes of people live side by side. It is called Pimlico, and it lies between Victoria Station, Buckingham Palace Road, and the Thames River. Small but heterogeneous, the district provided a convenient focus for my work. It is also an area with a great deal of charm: it has one of the few remaining London street markets, and it quarters the Queen's Horse Guards who parade daily to the Palace. Although the neighborhood is undergoing substantial redevelopment and renovation, for the time being the majority of its Victorian row houses have been spared.

After my return to Chicago, André Schiffrin at Pantheon encouraged me to photograph and interview a cross-section of the population of an American city to serve as a comparison to the London study. I looked for a heterogeneous neighborhood in Chicago that would be comparable to Pimlico, and chose Lincoln Park, one of the most mixed districts in Chicago. But in order to find as wide a cross-section as I did in Pimlico, I had to extend the official boundaries of the neighborhood, which were quite large already. So, in fact, my Chicago sample comes not exclusively from Lincoln Park, but rather from a much larger geographic area.

The procedure for carrying out my project was roughly the same in both cities. In London, with kind assistance from several community institutions, including a day care center, a prenatal clinic, and a doctor's office (please see Acknowledgments), I was able to recruit volunteer families for subjects, by putting up illustrated notices explaining my project and intent. The fact that the Arts Council of Great Britain had given me a grant probably legitimitized the project in many people's eyes. Everyone I photographed either signed up in this manner or was later referred to me by those already photographed. The voluntary aspect of this procedure was important psychologically to me, because starting out with willing subjects put all of us at ease. Having been invited into people's castles, first and foremost I wanted to photograph the families respectfully. This partly had to do with the social pressures to be polite in a polite country. More important, it was knowing how easy it is to take unkind advantage of one's subject with a camera, and not wanting to do that.

To my mind, photographing "respectfully" entailed a certain photographic procedure which allowed the families to put their best foot forward in the old portrait-studio tradition. All families had an appointment to be photographed. They could prepare in any way they chose, without instructions from me (with the exception of two policemen and a soldier, whom I asked to wear their uniforms). They could clean or not clean their houses in advance. If a preference for background was stated by the family, I respected it, lighting conditions permitting. My aim was to produce a photograph that would be pleasing to both the family and myself.

All families received as a "thank you" copies of the photographs I thought were the strongest images. Usually I gave each family two or three different shots. Inexplicably, most often the photograph I liked best was the photograph they liked best. In instances where either the family or I was dissatisfied with the results, I rephotographed the family (although it was not always easy to get polite people to say they didn't like their photograph!).

My decision to interview the families was made after I had completed the group of London portraits. It came from the realization that the photographs on their own left out too much information, including the interesting remarks people had made to me in passing. The photographs also raised too many questions, such as "Who are these people?" "Where did they come from?" "What are some of their concerns?" So six months after I had made the photographs, I returned to the families with my tape recorder.

Of the comments elicited in the interview, those of chief interest to me were the family's remarks about their own photographs. By asking families, "Is this photograph a fair description of you?" or "Would strangers get the right idea of you from this photograph?" they got a chance to identify with or disassociate themselves from their photograph. The discussion of the photograph, in addition to providing a vehicle for talking about themselves, pointed out the differences between self-image and a photographer's image, an area of great interest to me. (It would have been in a similar spirit to submit my edited interviews to the families for their comments. But unfortunately the mechanics and time needed to do this made the procedure impossible.)

I tried to standardize my approach to all the families, so that the differences between photographs are mostly a matter of details which necessitate careful looking on the part of the viewer in order to be detected. Looking becomes a game of sorts. More specifically, I used a camera with one almost "normal" lens, pointed it straight at the subjects at a "normal" angle, and used "normal-looking" lighting, even when flash was used. I also tried to minimize distortion. Besides often being kinder to the subject, a lack of distortion *seemingly* removes the photographer further from the picture. That is not to say the photographer is not there, operating in a self-conscious way. She is definitely there, but in a less obvious way. The picture does not scream, "Look what the photographer has done!" and the viewer can get on with the business of looking at the photograph. This is what I want viewers to do—to look carefully.

In looking at these photographs, the details one can glean serve as clues about the people. They are only hints or suggestions of people. Coupled with the family's own comments about their photograph, I hope they are not misleading suggestions. In the final analysis, the photographs are more about appearances—the physical look of things, as well as how people are willing to be seen by strangers. If how a person presents himself for a photograph says something about the person, then these photographs speak of the people in them.

While doing the Chicago portion of this book, certain cultural differences became apparent early on. They are differences which do not necessarily show up in the photographs but which forced me to vary my procedure slightly. Most noticeable was a certain discomfort many Americans seemed to feel in front of the camera. I work quite slowly, using a large camera and a tripod. In London I had successfully asked families to sit still for long exposures. In Chicago this was often an impossible request. After many unsatisfactory results I was obliged to purchase a very strong flash unit which meant it was no longer necessary to ask my subjects to sit still for long exposures. One possible explanation of the American attitude towards being photographed might be that the widespread use of Polaroids and Instamatics in America has made photography an instantaneous event, to be got over within a split second.

Whatever discomfort Americans seemed to feel in front of the camera was definitely lacking before the tape recorder. Compared to their English counterparts, most of my American subjects were at ease while being interviewed. They came alive at this point. In fact, their lack of inhibition in talking meant that limiting the interview to thirty or forty minutes was often difficult.

And finally, the last but perhaps most curious difference in carrying out the two portions of the project was the difficulty of recruiting volunteer families in Chicago. Whether it is because of fear or lack of trust of the outside world, Americans seem to be less willing to let an outsider in, even when one comes well recommended by neighbors and friends.

The assumption behind this book has been that ordinary people are interesting, unique, and worthy of our attention, especially if given a large enough platform from which they can show themselves to others. My efforts throughout have been to give them this platform.

LONDON

ALICE AND BEN WILLIAMS

MR. WILLIAMS: Retired clerk, department store

(Mr. Williams not interviewed)

Mrs. Williams: I'm eighty. My husband is eighty-seven. And I've been in Pimlico all me life. I was born in Buckingham Palace Road, along here. My father was born in Liverpool. He's Irish, you see. And my mother was born— oh dear, past Parliament Street. And there was six children. My father was a cabdriver, you see. Had his own cab. And he died at thirty-six. My mother married again. She had seven children by him. So really there was fourteen of us. Very nice family, all of us.

My husband worked at Army-Navy Stores all his life, Victoria Street. Export clerk. He worked from the age of sixteen right up till he was pensioned off. We had six sons, but two died. Yes, two of my sons are taxi drivers, and another son works at Watney's. Been there ever since he was a boy. And Benny works at the Army-Navy Stores, where his father worked, ever since he was nineteen. He's fifty-five now. I had the four boys in the Second World War. Thank God, they all come home safe.

Now Freddy's got five children and Jerry's got three children. Harry's got three children. And Benny's not married, you see. So I've got eleven grandchildren and two great-grandchildren.

Things around here is altered now. We used to live in a little street when the King died, when old King Edward died. Well, there was about twenty-four houses down there, and the Queen sent my mother and all of us a beautiful card, you know, because the street was so well decorated when he died and they passed by it. It was a lovely little street. We used to in fact help one another, you know. If anybody was out of work and had nothing, we'd put sort of tuppence or thruppence each and get him a dinner. It's different all together now. The surroundings, everywhere you go now they're pulling down houses and putting these high towers in.

Well, I worked up till I was seventy, really. Cleaner, you know, office cleaner. At the airways along here and then at the coastal station for nineteen years and never got a penny when I left. I've worked hard all me life, since I was twelve.

But I've had a good life, you know—I mustn't grumble. Because we don't want for nothing. We get by and we have everything we want really. I've got very good sons. They don't see us go short of anything.

I'm a Catholic. I'm not a bad person, you know. I believe in God and that. The priest comes every Friday and gives us Holy Communion. My husband's a Protestant, but he's been christened a Catholic two months ago. Well, I wanted it. I feel happier now because if anything happens to us we'd be both together, you know.

My husband is the same today as when I married him fifty-eight years ago. He's always been a good husband. In fact, you'd never hear him swear. Of course, I used to with the kids. And he's good to the children. Never interfered or knocked them about like some people do. He's been a wonderful man all his life.

THREE WISHES:
All I wish for is good health and to be happy, you know, and carry on and have the strength to look after my husband. That's all I wish for. I wish for nothing else.

ABOUT THE PHOTOGRAPH:
Mrs. Williams: Oh, they'd know me. Anybody see this they'd know it was me, yes. And Ben, they'd know him as well. I think it's a beautiful photo that. . . . I've got two or three nice little frocks, you know, and I put one on. It's so homely, isn't it? I think it's a beautiful photo of both of us, you know, sitting like that. And it's real life. I've never seen a photo like this.

MRS. PHYLLIDA CROOKSHANK
CHILDREN: ANTONIA, CHARLES

I was born in Somerset in the West Country. I left there when I was married, age nineteen, and after five years in the country, we came to London. That was about five years ago. I like it here.

My father was a retired army officer. He fought in the First World War and had lived in India. We were a country family. He retired long before I was born. He was sixty when I was born, so he was quite elderly. No, things were different in those days. They had more time for leisure, I think, and didn't have to work, unlike us now. As a child, I spent most of the time climbing trees and building fires and riding ponies and all the things I don't do any more. I miss it, and I miss it for my children, too, because I'd like them to be doing the things that I did, particularly Charles. He's rather too Londony. I'd rather prefer boys to be brought up in the country. I try to take them out to the country as much as one can and take them down to my mother in Dorset so they can get a bit of air.

I am hoping the children will go to a private school; public school as we call it. It is a better education if you can afford it, but it is so expensive now, and it's very difficult to know what the fee is going to be when they eventually go. Oh, yes, it's still better than the state education, I think. I think it teaches us a lot of things other than just lessons . . . how to get on with people and put up with other people's habits, because you all have to live together. And also it teaches them games and things like that that they all have to play together, not to be quite so selfish. I wasn't quite seven when I went to boarding school, which actually is much too early. But my children will be going at eight—well, the boy will be going at eight and a half and Antonia probably not until she's twelve.

The class system in Britain? I don't think one puts oneself in any class. I think other people put you in a class, really. . . . One just is, if you call it a class, that you're born in and your friends are. If you're feeling reasonably and hopefully secure in whatever you're doing, you don't have to talk about it. You don't even think about it. This is why it's not a rude question to ask one's class. It's just a difficult question.

THREE WISHES:
Goodness, I think probably just to be happy for the rest of one's life and to find somebody else to be happy with, I suppose, and to have a proper family instead of being on my own. I think other wishes stem from that. Yes, ultimately, I would like to settle down again and have sort of a reasonable home like everyone else does and not have to work and not have the responsibilities of looking after two children on my own. I'd quite like to lean on somebody else for a bit, but we'll see.

ABOUT THE PHOTOGRAPH:
Yes, I think it's a fair description of us, except Charles looks a bit glum. He usually smiles a bit more than that but he was rather self-conscious with the photograph. I think the children were a bit frightened on the day you came. But we all look quite happy together.

CAROL AND JOHN ROBINSON
CHILDREN: STUART, GREGORY

MR. ROBINSON: Professional soldier
MRS. ROBINSON: Part-time pub worker

Mr. Robinson: My family were ordinary working-class people in Sheffield, and we were never very well off when we were children. In fact, we were poor. But we always had enough to eat. My father worked for the same steel-works for thirty years. My mother works there now that we've all grown up.

Joining the army? I think it just happened to be a good thing at the time. I was eighteen. I had been making fishing rods for a small firm in Sheffield. I think I got talking to one or two people who had been in the army, you know, and then I went along and joined up for nine years. And I have been in for twelve now, and I will probably be in for another twelve. I think after people join the army they expect to be given a rifle, a Land Rover, and a flak jacket and be sent straight on to the streets of Ireland. But you know, you start right at the bottom with your short hair and a pair of baggy denims, and you know they cut you right down to size. You probably joined as individuals, but after an hour you're all sheep in the same barrack room.

I like the army. I think it's a very good and interesting life. We move every two or three years and you never get in a rut. I think for the children, for their sake, I'd like to be out of the army and have a house of our own—somewhere out of London into the country a bit, so they can see things like frogs and tadpoles and lizards.

Since I've been in the army there hasn't been a time of national emergency where we have to be on the defensive like we were during the last war. So it's difficult, with any intelligence, to appreciate that you're doing the country a lot of good. I don't think we are, to be quite honest. I think most people in the army look on Ireland or anywhere else we go as a personal experience—something to have done, something to see. I think we earn a lot of dollars for the country when we wear our tunics and the American tourists come and see us, but even that is just a joke. . . . There's no sort of national spirit here, as there is perhaps in America. We were all born during the war when the national spirit was riding high. But after the war it just generally declined.

After twenty-two years in the army you can go out on a pension. So I will only be forty-two, and obviously it's time to start again somewhere. I have no idea what I'll do. I have no qualifications for anything. I would like to see a bit more of the world, more in a tourist capacity. Eventually when the children are married and all, I would like to retire to a little cottage in the countryside and just read. And they'll come visit once a month.

Mrs. Robinson: I enjoy the army, but I don't like being split up for long periods. But then you get used to it after a time. . . . If we had enough money I would like to come out of the army, mainly I think because of the separations. I don't like being separated. Ireland is the worst. Very worrying, Ireland. The worst four months we've ever had.

When the children are old enough they'll go to boarding school, a private school where they stop and just come home for the holidays. The army pays towards this, which is a good thing. The children are quite bright. I think whatever they want to do they can go ahead, within reason, of course.

We're much the same as anybody else here. You know, do much the same, have our traditional Sunday dinner. We have a car, which most families have.

I work in a pub where I do the cooking, and sometimes do the shopping. I've always worked. I like working, but at the moment I would like to go back to being a telephonist. When the children grow up I will go back to working on the switchboard.

ABOUT THE PHOTOGRAPH:

Mrs. Robinson: Not often do I come home in that uniform, but I do think it's an excellent photo of the children.

Mrs. Robinson: I would like the uniform photograph in the book.

PEGGY WAINFERNS
CHILDREN: DONNA, CARL, SASCHA, OLIVER

We were rehoused by the council nearly four years ago—from Paddington. I don't like it here at all—no shopping center, no places for the children to play, too built-up.

I adore my children. I enjoy them, play with them, go with them, take them out, never mind about the housework, kids are only young once. Why should you do all the housework and keep the house nice when you can go out and enjoy yourself with the kids? They leave home so quickly you don't have them for long. So, I'm going to enjoy them while I've got them. They're mine.

I don't like sending my kids to schools. They don't get enough education in there. After five, we are forced to send our kids to school. It's a law. We have no choice. It's very wrong. You don't have them for very long anyways, so why should they make you send your child to school, which sometimes amounts up to as much as forty hours a week. You wouldn't send a child to work for forty hours a week.

I don't want discipline in school where they make children sit down all the time. They're not going to learn that way. They must have expression of speech and movement. They have a lot of freedom in this house, far more than any child I think. They're allowed to do most anything.

I don't have much to do with anybody here [Ebury Bridge Estate]. Well, I haven't found anybody really suitable because I've got four children and if they accept me they've got to accept my four kids. And most people don't like big families, you know, and mine are a bit boisterous.

If you haven't got a high income coming in, you've got to make do with what you've got. Some people can and some people can't, and I'm one who can. I don't owe anybody a ha'penny. Not one ha'penny. I don't have debts. I can't afford it.

I do get money from the government, but not a lot. And it is degrading. They must know how many children, who is the father here, does he give you this, does he give you that. It's so personal and there's no privacy. And they come here to check up on you even late at night. I've had them here at eight at night checking up.

Nearly two years ago, I became a Mormon. They do a lot for children. Even if they're babes in arms, they have a special room for them to play in and they have a good Sunday School for them and they're allowed to make an awful lot of noise and no child is ever refused. I mean if you go to church and you have not got your children, you are asked, "Where are your children?" They believe in family life.

THREE WISHES:
For my children, I would wish for a nice house in the country, plenty of trees, and some animals. Never mind about mom so much. It doesn't matter if it was a palace, as long as it was somewhere miles and miles away from anybody.

I would love some more children. I really would. But of course it's a question of money. I had the last three in two years and I think I've done a good job because they look well. I'd love another couple sons and another couple daughters and I think they would grow up fine strong people. I want my children to grow up and be honest. And that's it. That's a lot, you know. It's an awful lot.

When my kids grow up? I'm going to have a time of my own. My time. I shall go everywhere. I shall go abroad.

ABOUT THE PHOTOGRAPH:

I look too goody-goody good in the photograph. And I think it has too many feet. We should have put a cushion over some of them. I think we would make a good advertisement there for feet. . . . It's too ordered, you know. It looks as though we've just sat there, just posed for you.

Oliver: It's quite good really. I got a bit bigger since then and then my hair was all silver. I had short hair then. I don't like the wall because there are scribbles, as you can see. So much crayon on it that me mom went up the wall.

DORIS AND JIM ARMOUR
DOG: TEDDY

MR. ARMOUR: Accountant

Mr. Armour: It's our eleventh year in Pimlico now. An aunt of ours died and her property went on the market to the family and we got this house at a very low price. It has made a tremendous difference to our lives because otherwise we'd be struggling where we were before in the West End, paying rent. It's lovely here. We always wanted to live in the West End. This is just sufficiently near to the West End to enable us to do everything we like to do.

When we got the house, Pimlico was reckoned to be a slum area, a real low-class area. But there's a tremendous amount of money that has been poured into Pimlico. These speculators have made this place into the most fantastic living area that you could possibly imagine.

I was born in Peckham, which sounds rather, a bit working class. My father had a pub there. Well, I hated the pub right from the time I was a kid, you know. My father was all for me to be going into the business, but I didn't want to. So I left, we even had a row over it, and I went out on my own and started buying and selling things on the street. I always think how lucky I am to have got out of it all. But being born in a pub more or less, I still hate pubs. I go into one maybe twice a year on average.

Mrs. Armour: I was the second eldest of seven children. We had come to London from Liverpool, just after the strikes in 1926. I was ten years old. We lived in just one room, just off Waterloo, where Festival Hall is right now. My mother had a terrible time because we were so poor.

Mr. Armour: I'm an accountant. That was sheer luck too. In 1933, somebody had a whole lot of little bookkeeping jobs, and he offered them to me and he showed me how to do them. I managed to fiddle along doing these book-keeping jobs. Then I realized I didn't know anything about it and I started to buy little books on accountancy and so I more or less self-taught myself. And now I'm a practicing accountant.

The most interesting part of my life has been the fact that I was a voluntary police officer for twenty-four years at West End Central. Incidentally, I do support law and order to every extent and I believe in a strong police force. I think it's the only way any civilized community can carry on. It happened during the war; I thought I'd join the police in order to do my little bit. So I was on duty during the whole of the blitz in the West End, and that was a frightening experience. I remember walking down the street one day, you heard the bombs dropping and so on— and thinking how scared I was and that everybody else seemed to be very brave. I came across two chaps in a doorway who called out to me, "Oh hello, you seem to be very calm about all this." And I said, "Well, I'm scared as hell." They said, "That's why we're in here." And they were two regulars!

Mrs. Armour: I remember a lot about the war. My father died on the first day of the war. Had a heart attack and just died. He had to pass over a bridge at the station at Croydon. There were hundreds of children around the platforms wearing gas masks, waiting for trains. And it might have been seeing the children that triggered it off. I used to commute between the West End where I worked

---

ABOUT THE PHOTOGRAPH:

Mr. Armour: I didn't realize I looked so damned old. That's what beats me. My wife looks all right, but I look like a bloomin' old man. Strangers would think I'm a retired old so-and-so and I had a very charming young wife or something. . . . I've never even looked in the glass and thought I looked as bad as that. The dog comes out well.

Mrs. Armour: I'm pleased with the way it turned out. You can see who the painting is, I think. It's the Queen Mother. Well, she has a certain way of sitting, doesn't she, and dressing that's typically her. . . . I managed to do one painting a year for the past three years . . . but there's been so much else to do that I haven't done any since that.

and Croydon, where I lived. And that was quite hair-raising business. I saw the first bombs that fell in London when they fell on a perfumery factory in Croydon. I was in a garden and heard these planes coming over and I looked up. Suddenly these darn white things were·pouring out of them. They hit the factory and a lot of people were killed. And we saw them go over for D-Day. We didn't know it was D-Day. There were hundreds of gliders, all being towed over there, all in a straight line. Hundreds of them. It was a fantastic sight!

It was after the war that we had the children. And then things were very tight, even for five or six years later. Things were still rationed into the fifties, I think.

Mr. Armour: And today, oh, my goodness, compared to the old days people don't realize how well off they are.

ABOUT THE CHILDREN:
Mr. Armour: Our children are a lot freer than we were. They could do more or less what they wanted to, and that applies pretty well all over the country. For instance, my son suddenly said to me, "I'm going off to South Africa next month." Now at one time the father said, "Now you've got a jolly good job and you stick around here." And the son wouldn't have dared to defy his father. And the way we brought up the children I probably said, "You're much safer to stick around in a safe job," and left it to him to decide what to do. Well, he went off to Africa.

Both their mother and I pointed out to them that it was entirely up to them whether they became well-educated or whether they didn't. Whether they wanted to get amongst the rulers of the country or not—and when I said *rulers,* I mean all those in executive positions who run the country. They both started realizing that their schooling was entirely for themselves. Now one son is a zoologist and the other is a civil engineer. I think we've done very well, really, in the way we've brought them up.

JANET AND NICHOLAS WOOLLEY
CHILDREN: OLIVER, CASPER, BENEDICT

MRS. WOOLLEY: Full-time student in social work
MR. WOOLLEY: Radio newscaster and editor

Mr. Woolley: The best way to describe my origins would be to say Victorian middle-class ancestry, mercantile success in the late nineteenth century, and then really comparatively small success from then on, rather an inclination to let everything dissipate and fritter away. I think we're just really now the impoverished or relatively impoverished professional classes. The rest of my relations with whom I had close contact during the war were parsons, who notoriously are not particularly rich. So we never had any money.

My father was a naval officer for a time during the First World War, and then he was a commissioner of national savings. When I was young he went away to the war and died on the last day of the war—he died, he wasn't killed. He was an intelligent, able man, he lacked ambition, I think he may have been idle—I'm not sure—he had a good deal of charm, he was interested in acting, and a lot of those things I can see in myself. My mother is an ordinary conservative middle-class Christian, and although I'm not a Christian I can see a lot of that in myself, residual. So yes, I think I am the logical product of my parenthood.

My job at the BBC is the third job I tried, the third of three related jobs, first of which was preaching, the second of which was acting, the third of which was broadcasting, journalism included. I cover stories as a reporter, more often interviewing major participants; I present news programs, and I also sit at the other side of the desk and act as an editor. My job is important because, although I think this country is supposed to be well-informed and sophisticated, there is a great deal to be done, both in the long term and in the short, to tell people what's going on and allow different points of view about those events to be aired.

I had thought of being a priest since, I suppose, sometime in my teens. So I went to university, theological school, and I simply found at the end of two years—we had to preach various sermons in little baby churches, daughter churches in the wilds of Somerset—that I wasn't preaching to these five or six good ladies and laborers who came to evensong. I was preaching to myself, trying to convert myself. So then I went off and did the next job I was most interested in, acting. And I went to work for a year in a repertory theater, which I enjoyed very much, and I only stopped doing it because really I couldn't afford to live on eight pounds, or as I rose, ten pounds a week.

I sometimes wonder whether we were right to have had children. Perhaps all parents feel this way. But life for our children is going to be a great deal more difficult and unpleasant than it has been for us. I fear annihilation, and if not annihilation, strangulation through the limitation of resources. But more likely annihilation as a result of the political and military struggles that arise out of these difficulties.

I think I'm following really in a modified form the same ideals as my parents did. I would like to see my children strong enough individually to feel free and to act freely while securely enough fixed in their society, both on the small scale of their home or their village or their street and on the large scale of their nation, and perhaps the world, to fit in and to contribute to the actual culture as well. I mean, it's a combination of individual satisfaction and contribution and how to achieve this balance. If there was one gift I had to give them it would be self-knowledge, at an early age. I know I didn't have it.

Mrs. Woolley: My own family? I would have thought it was very much middle-of-the-road, solid middle-class. My mom, in fact, as far as working went, didn't do anything, certainly in a paid capacity. As we grew older and more independent, she became a local councilor, and she took a very great interest in everything that was going on in the village. My father worked for Barclays Bank. He went in at the age of sixteen at the very bottom possible level and spent all his life working for the bank and ended up as a local director, which was a good solid job to have. Many people would say, "Goodness, all your life with Barclays Bank!" but I think it did give him enormous satisfaction.

When my mother married she took with her into marriage a young woman who had been in fact a nursery maid in her father's—my grandfather's—household, who then in turn became nanny to all of us. She very much thought of us as her children in a very possessive way. It was not really a job at all. It was her life. And she was always there. In fact, she still is there now living with my father.

I wouldn't have had a nanny for my children. I think we wanted to feel that our children learned what our ways were, direct as it were, with nobody in between.

We have spent ten years arguing whether we really want to be in London or whether we want to be in the country. We've got now to the halfway stage where we do have a place in the country, one hundred miles away, that we go to for part of the week. And although that has a lot of advantages, it also puts extra strains on living. Simply having four nights in one place and three nights in another makes it difficult to get anything done at either end, and it's always rather the feeling that you're living out of a suitcase that never gets unpacked.

My ideas about wanting a career have been creeping up. For the first seven years of marriage, as it were, I didn't have any difficulty in putting the children first. And although I did a part-time job pretty well all the time, the job was very much secondary and had to fit in with the children. And then, I suppose in the last couple of years I began to feel—not exactly the maternal instinct had run out, but that if I concentrated only on the children I couldn't give them the same sort of things that I'd been giving them. I mean emotionally.

Whether this was something in me, or the boys were getting to be more independent and they didn't need me so much, I'm not sure.

I would still say I'm not a career woman. That suggests to me someone who has driving ambition to do whatever it is she is doing. And I don't think I have that enormous pushing feeling. What I want from a job is some sort of nondomestic satisfaction.

Like Nick, I can't think of anything more useful than self-knowledge. I would simply like each one of my children to find what suits him best, what they can really put most of themselves into. I tremendously envy my brother, who from the moment he could speak, knew and said that he wanted to be a farmer. And he went on saying this although nobody in the family farmed and there seemed to be no possibility of his farming. But he made it in the end because he knew that was the one thing he burned to do. But most of us never have that singleminded feeling.

ABOUT THE PHOTOGRAPH:

Mr. Woolley: I think strangers could make certain logical deductions possibly. Well, if they look at a grandfather clock and plates hanging on the wall and things, they say, well, they are of a certain sort of background. And they might guess or deduce right. But as for knowing whether I was a bomb-throwing IRA man, I don't think you could tell.

I can see things in the children that are characteristic. I mean it's characteristic of Casper, in a sense, to play the clown, or Ben, to have been caught at the wrong moment, and that Oliver does have the sort of unwinking gaze of the very young.

Mrs. Woolley: I don't like the photographs. I find the children looking incredibly unnatural. I think your sort of aim really was to set people up formally, and within that aim I would find it difficult to feel comfortable. I'd feel much happier if you could take us swinging from a tree or something. We're not formal, and I think we all go a bit goofy when we're lined up to be shot.

I agree with Nick that it would be very difficult on the basis of the people to get any impression at all. There are the middle-class trappings if you like, but I am not sure nowadays anything is proved by trappings. And just looking at me, I think I look much more soft and motherly than I ever felt in my life.

CATHERINE AND DOUGLAS HUMPHREYS

MR. HUMPHREYS: Retired employee of the Royal Household, Buckingham Palace

Mr. Humphreys: Before age eighteen I was right back in the Sussex village. I had just one sister. She went to a place in Kent, in service, which in those days was the only jobs open for girls, as kitchen maid or parlormaid, which you see on your television in *Upstairs, Downstairs*, which is absolutely truth. My father was sort of agricultural laborer and part-time bricklayer.

Like many youth at that period of time, you traveled to London to see what London is like. You think the place is paved with gold, but you have a terrific misunderstanding. My first job in London was in the Oxford and Cambridge Club in Pall Mall as a page. I worked there for many years. But I found I couldn't get any further than sort of waiter because the old staff were there and they didn't want to lose their jobs and they sort of resented it. So I just left.

During the war I got a job making wings for planes, in the factory. I thought I might as well join up, enlist and be secure, which I did. And that was another four and a half years out of my life, in the army. And after the war, in 1946, you had to struggle for a job. I registered at the Labour Exchange. I just walked in calmly one morning and the clerk there said, "Just the fellow we want." He had two jobs. One was porter at Buckingham Palace and one at Westminster Hospital. I chose Buckingham Palace. Now even today I don't know whether I chose the right job or not. In a hospital you come across more of humanity. That's what my aim's always been through life. To meet people humanly.

I was at Buckingham Palace for nineteen years. One of the most interesting episodes was the state funeral of Sir Winston Churchill, when all the heads who attended the funeral were invited back to Buckingham Palace for a cold buffet. I was entertaining myself a few moments with Mr. Khrushchev. Oh yes, now he had two bodyguards and an interpreter with him. I took off his greatcoat and I felt the eyes of those burly guards. I hung his greatcoat up and I said to the interpreter, "Just tell your two men to relax. I'm on duty on the occasion of Her Majesty's Royal Household." And I added, "One day I would like to pay a visit to your country, sir." And afterwards Mr. Khrushchev came back to what was then called the morning room, and I helped him on again with his coat. He thanked me through his interpreter and actually shook hands.

Mrs. Humphreys: I came from a little village in Norfolk. As my husband said, in those days there was nothing really much in the villages where you lived except going into service. And I didn't particularly want to go into service. My mother was a caretaker in a big house down there, and my father was the gardener, and he used to work on the golf course, you see. There were eleven of us, eleven children.

I came to London when I was fifteen. My sister and my three brothers were up in London, so my mother was quite happy about it. My sister was at the Oxford and Cambridge Club as a pastry cook and she got me a job there with her. And that's where I met Mr. Humphreys. It was a very nice life, club life, really. You'd get out every afternoon and then you'd have the staff dances once a year and you could always go around to the other club dances because my brothers worked in several of the other clubs.

I remember the General Strike in 1926 when Mr. Humphreys was out of work. They were hard days, but they were happy days. You had no money, but everybody made their own entertainment. We never even had a wireless in those days. Today everybody's got everything they want, but they're still not happy.

ABOUT THE PHOTOGRAPH:

Mr. Humphreys: I'm over seventy, so I can't expect to look twenty-five. So to me that's a jolly good job you've done.

Mrs. Humphreys: It is. He looks like the Prince of Wales there, doesn't he? I mean the Prince of Wales that's gone, the Duke of Windsor. That's very good. It's as we are.

KATHLEEN AND ROBERT ORSBORN
(parents of Ron Orsborn)
CHILDREN: RONALD, GRAHAM, DAVID, SUSAN

MRS. ORSBORN: Cashier
MR. ORSBORN: Auctioneer

Mrs. Orsborn: In my street people smile, say good morning, hello, always somebody. I was born here. My mother was, my father too, over the bridge, Ebury Bridge, in the real Pimlico.

Mr. Orsborn: We went to school together. I can remember her from four or five.

Mrs. Orsborn: Everybody played in a group. And everybody knew everybody else's mom and dad. But you could knock at people's doors, you know, and say, "Could I have a drink of water?" or "Could I go to the toilet?" And they didn't mind whose kids it was. It was friendly.

Mr. Orsborn: Oh, it was lovely.

Mrs. Orsborn: But the kids today, the poor little devils can't even play in the yard. The area has changed.

Mr. Orsborn: It's the people. The people are better off now.

Mrs. Orsborn: I think its gone to their heads. You know, they become la-di-da and they aren't really. I mean we're better off. Let's face it. We were poor. But it hasn't changed us. But nine out of ten people it changes. I mean good luck to anybody to better themselves. I'm not against that. I wanted better for my children, and I hope they will want better for their children. But at the same time I don't want them to change basically. I don't want them to forget what they are.

I want my children to be loving and to be kind and to be fair. And to be friendly. Really truly friendly. Look after each other. I'm sure if the Lord took me, my boys would look after their sister. Or their grandmothers. We go away at weekend and I say to David, "Will you look after your grandmother?" She's ninety-seven. And he doesn't grumble.

You know, we were brought up during the war. Let's face it. I think that was a fabulous time anyway. I mean that really brought out the best in everybody. I stayed, I didn't evacuate. In the morning you got up and the All Clear went and you called across the road, "Are you all right, love?"

Mr. Orsborn: There's not a dozen around here our age that are still around here.

Mrs. Orsborn: The girls my age, they married Canadians or Americans and went abroad. And others got council houses and moved out to new towns. Today to buy a house in London you've got to be Rothschild's daughter or something.

THREE WISHES:
Mrs. Orsborn: I don't want a great big pools win. I would like a little bit more money each week and no bills. Really, if this inflation carries on, we're going to be right back where we started. And I want to go around the world. Ah, that's a wonderful wish, that is.

My life now is my grandchildren. I look after them in the mornings, you see, while their moms go out and earn a few shillings. Then when they come home and collect the children, I go out to work in the afternoons. But I'm happy that way. I don't want to go out a lot. But I do look forward to a holiday. Oh, I feel like a millionaire when I go!

ABOUT THE PHOTOGRAPH:
Mrs. Orsborn: I don't think that picture captures what we are really like. We look like a load of snobs there, don't we? We're much happier than that picture shows. A really close-knit family.

David: I don't like standing in front of the camera grinning, you know? I think a photo should be taken by surprise. These posing things, you can never get the real thing. You see the Royal Family like that, don't you. No, the only way to get a picture is by surprise.

DAPHNE AND RON ORSBORN
CHILD: ALLAN

MR. ORSBORN: Full-time student

Mr. Orsborn: My father was born in the building behind this one. My mother was born in the street next to this one. My two grans live here. We're a very close-knit and very happy family. I think it has to do with living together in this area. I've never left, except when I went in the army, of course. In fact, when I was in the army I used to hitchhike miles to get back here for weekends. I have never thought of moving anywhere else.

It used to be much better. You could play football in the street, you could let the dog run. Now it's terrible. All antique shops. You go over the bridge, just across the road, Churchill Gardens, Abbot's Manor Estates—rabbit hutches. I don't like it. But I'm going to end up there, obviously, because this house we're renting is coming down very soon and we'll have to be rehoused somewhere.

All there is around here really is the pub and the club. That's it. The cinemas are all gone except one, you know, and that's a pound to get in now. I wish this place could be just like it was when I was a bit younger. It was a smashing area to live in. You know, now they stick the old-timers in the skyscrapers and they've had it. You don't know your next-door neighbor. At least with a garden you can shout across the wall to somebody. This Christmas we got cards from the people both sides of us. And that's because we are in a house. Last Christmas when we lived in a flat we got nothing from our neighbors. Ridiculous.

I'm on a course, a general engineering course, mechanical fitting. It's a government training thing, and it'll give me a trade all right. Initially I wanted to go to sea, to be a marine engineer. But I was color-blind. I couldn't see a blue buoy on a black background. And that was that. Then I volunteered for the army and stayed nearly ten years. I was very lucky. I was a sportsman. I was a rugby player in the winter, an athlete in the summer, and in the autumn I was a swimmer. So I did very little army work and a great deal of sport.

I'd like to give my children as much as I got. I'd like to have enough money to keep them well, you know, so they don't want for anything. And I want them to be men. You know, the pouffs that you get around here. Bloody terrible.

THREE WISHES:
Health for the family, security, and happiness. What's security? I'd like to have a house that's mine and be able to say, "Right, I'm going to live here for the next fifty years." At the moment it might be seven years or three months before they turn around and say, "Away you go." That's not security, really.

Mrs. Orsborn: I come from Kent. I used to work in a supermarket. I had all sorts of ideas about working on a farm or joining the navy. But it didn't work out, so I stayed at the supermarket and made a lot of friends there. But there was another girl who worked there and she wanted to join the army. I thought it would be quite exciting, so I joined her and we went in together.

I met my husband in the army. When I got married, I moved here. I had been in the army for about seven months.

ABOUT THE CHILDREN:
I wouldn't force them to do anything they didn't want to. I'd rather that they made up their own minds. But I'd rather they bettered themselves. I wouldn't want them to roam the streets, you know, being hippies. I'll do my best to encourage them to do better things, like to be a doctor or something like that.

ABOUT THE PHOTOGRAPH:
Mr. Orsborn: The photograph looks natural, I suppose. But people would have to come to one of my parties to find out what we're really like. . . . I would have painted the doorstep if I'd known you were going to take a picture of it. And the lump is now a second boy, so we're very happy.

CAROL AND MICHAEL COOPER
CHILDREN: KATE, LORIEN

MR. COOPER: Sculptor

. . . . . Moved to the country . . . . .

LILLIAN AND WILLIAM GILBY
(parents of Keith Gilby)

MR. GILBY: Retired greengrocer

(Mr. Gilby not interviewed)

Mrs. Gilby: My mother was a war widow because my father was killed in the First World War. We were five children. She'd clean offices in Whitehall in the morning and then she used to clean ladies' flats during the day while we were at school, and then again office-cleaning at night. So we didn't see much of her. My grandfather and grandmother always looked after us when she went to work at night. She was a very good mother.

I think that children have got a better life today. But I'm glad I lived in the way I did. I mean we lived in a big house in Cumberland Street, and my mother was so poor we had no cloth on our stairs and every Saturday morning we had to clean these stairs down. But I was very happy.

I think we were happier because we had a lovely mother. I think that makes a difference, don't you think so? Then I had an elder brother, and he went to work at Watney's when he was fourteen and he used to give us all a penny or a ha'penny—you know, pocket money, as he called it. He was like a father to us. And then I can always remember my mother saying, "I may never come home again, but whatever you do, keep the children to Sunday School." My mother went at fifty-five. In 1941.

My husband lived in Victoria, where the Victoria Palace is now. Well, he sold fruit in a stall in Warwick Way, and I couldn't pass without him saying, "No apples today?" I used to say, "No money." And he'd say, "Oh yeah?" And I used to get the apples for nothing. I worked in a coffee shop in Rochester Row. He said, "Will I see you tonight?" And I said, "I don't finish till seven." And then I went out with him.

We got married and had seven sons and two daughters. Now I have twelve grandchildren. During the war Pimlico was badly bombed. I had all the children with me, none of them evacuated, because I couldn't bear to part with them. I thought, if one goes, we all go together. The welfare lady used to come and say, "We'll get you a little place all together." Well, I still wouldn't go, because my mother had a weak heart and I didn't like to leave her either. So we used to go into the cellars at night. We put beds down there, you know, and made a bedroom of it.

We were a very close family. We all used to get together in 1940 and sit and knit. You know, the church used to give us the wool and we used to sit and make helmets, mittens, and scarves for the soldiers.

Ever since 1940, I've always minded somebody else's child, fostered children from the welfare. Well, that helped put shoes on my children's feet. I was a registered Westminster foster mother. Now I'm too old to have any more. My husband hasn't worked for years because he's got rheumatoid arthritis. He gets his war disability pension and his old-age pension, and I get my old-age pension. We manage. Yes, we manage.

I like living here and I wouldn't want to go away. We've got the center over there. We can go over there and meet people. You can go every morning and fold letters and sew buttons on cards and fold tissue paper, and you can earn a pound for the week. My husband goes with me. He likes it very much. And we go to the little Methodist Church over there. You know, a lot of our neighbors have left London. Some bought little houses and retired, some of them were old and went. But some are still around. That's why I like going to the little Methodist Church, because I can see them there.

THREE WISHES:
Just peace. I never wanted money, as long as I could pay my way. And good health. I don't want anything else.

ABOUT THE PHOTOGRAPH:
Mrs. Gilby: Oh yes, that's how I've always looked. Oh yes, people would know that is me. My husband always looks the same. He's always looked old 'cause you see he won't wear teeth. I don't know why he won't get any teeth.

MARGARET AND KEITH GILBY
CHILD: KENNETH

MR. GILBY: Foreman in auction house

Mr. Gilby: There's no place like home. I was born here. I've always lived in Westminster, and I don't think I would want to move out of it. As my mother told you, I had a lot of brothers and sisters. It was terrific. Really terrific. Three of us have stayed in the area. I've got one brother who's in Scotland. He's a policeman, and he married a girl up there from when he was in the army. But he still comes home for Christmas. And the others have more or less gone to where their wives were living, sort of the outskirts of London, where they've had a chance to buy their own places. Because to buy property in London is impossible. We've always been close, and we've more or less kept contact with everybody.

Yes, I remember when my father was a greengrocer. I still remember going to market with him, going to Covent Garden, going up there to bring home the salad or the fruit. His heart and soul was in his stall. It was in Warwick Way. And that stall has become mine now. I've got the license for it. My father's father passed that on to my father and then it's come to me, and now, if I like, I could pass it on to Kenneth.

I did have the stall out before I got the job that I've got now. When my dad came down to the stall I used to say, "Dad, look after the stall. I'm going for a cup of tea." Because I knew it was his pride and glory to be there. And when I used to come back to the stall he'd have the apples and you'd see they'd be polished up. He knew more on how to display a stall than I think anybody I knew. And you could see his face in the scales. I guarantee he had the cleanest pair of scales in Westminster.

The stall is empty at the moment because I've got a position with the top auctioneer in the country. I'm a foreman over six men. They really look after their staff. And when they look after us you've got to consider them. I'd like my son to go into the job I've got now, if he wanted to. He'd have a career for the rest of his life.

I would like to see him go to college. I was fifteen when I left school. I always intended to go into the print. That was my one ambition. But when I got into the print, I found that being closed in all day long, I wasn't satisfied. I passed my apprenticeship out and then I left. I come up to work for the barrow boys for a while and then I got the job I've got now. It worked out very very well.

I met Margaret when I had me fruit stall. It started off that Margaret come along while I was unloading a load of empties from the stall. And we got to actually talking and we went out for the evening. And I said to her, "Well, we're getting married." And out of the blue she said, "Yes." I was more surprised myself than I think she was.

Mrs. Gilby: I was about three when I came to London from Stockport, Cheshire. I like the North very much. I grew up in the East End of London. It was all right apart from my father died when I was seven.

I like being a mother. It's something I've always wanted. I mean we always tried to have children. After seven years of waiting Kenneth finally come along. And then it took us three months to really believe that I was pregnant.

I know a few other mothers around here, but not an awful lot. I mainly go up to his mom. And there's a girl that lives up in a flat where Keith's mom lives and I've become very friendly with her. We see each other every day of the week. One day I go around there and the next day she comes around to me. She has a little girl thirteen months. She's quite a good friend, really.

THREE WISHES:
I would like a little sister for Kenneth. And a house with a garden for him to play with. And to continue living a happy life. That's about all.

ABOUT THE PHOTOGRAPH:
Mr. Gilby: The photograph is a perfect photo of the boy. It's very much like us.
Mrs. Gilby: I quite agree with Keith.

MARGARET AND RICHARD BRANDT
CHILDREN: EDMUND, CHARLOTTE

MR. BRANDT: Accountant

Mr. Brandt: I became an accountant because my father was a chartered accountant. I was at university and didn't know what I was going to do. Well, my father walked into the bathroom one morning—and if you're lying prone in the bath you find yourself at a disadvantage when somebody's laying down the laws of your future life—and then he said, "If you can't make up your mind, you may just as well be a chartered accountant as anything else." And he arranged for me to be articled to the firm he belonged to, and that's how it happened.

Mrs. Brandt: I was a London suburbs girl. I was born in Ealing. During the war my father took us to the country. And then we came back and lived very much in a dormitory suburb called Bexley Heath.

I can be summed up as a product of the welfare state. That's totally me. If the 1944 Education Act hadn't been, I probably wouldn't, almost certainly wouldn't, have gone to university. That Act opened up secondary grammar school education. It also provided grants for the people who couldn't get scholarships but were still capable of going on to university. So it meant that I went off to a red-brick university, Reading, where I did modern languages.

Question: Is the class system loosening up?

Mr. Brandt: You must not think of the class system as being rigid. It is defined, but people move. You move by making money to enable you to equip yourself to live in a different class. You are never accepted in that class, but your children are. Margaret's family is an example. Her father started out on the factory bench and became a mechanical engineer in the Ministry of Supply. He came up, as it were, and made good. Her mother came from shopkeeping background in West London. Margaret was brought up in a totally different and alien way. She was educated and was allowed to get away from her background.

ABOUT THE CHILDREN:

Mr. Brandt: I hope the children will be happy. I think it's more important to be happy than to be successful. I do not wish to live my own life or to correct the mistakes of my own life through my children, which is how some people may perhaps look at it.

Mrs. Brandt: Certainly, at this stage, what I ask of them is that they will develop their own ability to its full extent. I mean, if one of them decides he wants to do woodwork rather than anything else, then please will he go on and become a master carpenter and not stop at apprentice stage. I would like that they make the most of what they have. Then they can do what they want.

THREE WISHES:

Mrs. Brandt: I think one is more of a prayer, that my children will grow up healthy, wealthy, wise, if you like. I suppose most mothers have got a fear that something will happen to a child. A general wish that the world would come to its senses and that some sort of stability would happen in all forms, again for the children's future. That sounds much deeper than it's meant to be because, in fact, it hasn't stopped me from recently bringing another one into the world. And nothing for myself except to lose weight and stop going gray.

Mr. Brandt: I would wish for time, enough time to do everything I want to do. The next wish would definitely be that places wouldn't change. Whenever I go back to places I knew, I find these horrid little developments. And my last wish would be fewer other people.

ABOUT THE PHOTOGRAPH:

Mr. Brandt: I must say I come out looking rather like a model for one of the American primitive painters, one of those long, thin Puritans, the archetypal New Englander.

Mrs. Brandt: We look reasonably happy.

Mr. Brandt: We look surprisingly well integrated in regard to everything. Incidentally, the painting above is of our street in Pimlico.

PAMELA DIXON
CHILDREN: PHILLIP, PAUL

I've been in London since I was sixteen. I come from Blackpool. It's good old Lancashire. You won't believe it, but I was the thirteenth child. My father was a precision fitter and my mother couldn't work because she was an invalid. We used to go to Sunday School and I used to pray that my mother would get better. Naturally, she never did get better.

Given the opportunity and God be willing and God rest my parents and that, I don't think I would have come up to London. I think I would have stayed in the North with the family. But you know, when I became of age to go out to work, there wasn't a great deal of work. So I came to London with a girlfriend. I just wanted to get out in the world. I never got the right opportunities to get on, admittedly.

I worked in some good places and I've done some various kinds of jobs. Well, I was an assistant cook for a starter. And then I went to work in the theater, the Carlton Tower, in the Haymarket. I first started there as an usherette, and then I got put in charge of sales, which was a promotion, you know. And if it wasn't for the fact that I moved out of London for a while, I still would have most likely been there and may have been the manageress.

I liked working at the Carlton because we used to have all these fantastic film stars, you know, especially Bing Crosby. I really love his singing. And his films—fantastic! He's my sweetheart, he is. Oh yes, I mean we had premieres all the time. And I had the opportunity once to see the Queen to her seat, which was fantastic, absolutely fantastic, especially when she gives you her gloves to hold. I was in charge of the Royal Box that evening, and I thought it was lovely.

I've been on my own since Paul was thirteen weeks old. Quite a long time. I mean I have to succumb to social security. I get a family allowance for Phillip, and like everybody else who has got small children, I get milk tokens. But it's not a great deal of money. My flat is a council flat. We've only got the one gas fire in the whole of the flat. I can't, say, go out and get a nice piece of meat for a Sunday. In fact, I think the last time we had meat was Christmas, two months ago. And that was a chicken that was given to me for Christmas. But we do manage.

Phillip goes to the nursery in the afternoons, just across the bridge there. He goes from one to four, which is a help in one way but a hindrance in another way, because it's not long enough. It doesn't give me a chance to go out and get a job.

I've taught Paul to do housework purposely, because I think it's a good thing for a child to learn housework, to learn how to cook, how to look after themselves. Because naturally I'm not going to be around all the time, and once he knows how to, say, cook a meal and wash up and clean up, wash his clothes and so forth, then I know he'll be all right. You see a lot of tramps walking the streets. They're tramps not because they want to be. They're tramps because they don't know how to look after themselves properly.

THREE WISHES:
Paul: I'd like to wish for a big house with a garden, a boat, and permission to have a pet.

ABOUT THE PHOTOGRAPH:

Ms. Dixon: I like the outside photograph in one sense because it doesn't look as though it's poseful. Do you understand? And because that shows part of the area where we live.

Paul: I like the outside photograph because mommy's sitting down, you've got a good view of the area, I'm holding Phillip in me arms because I like to pick Phillip up.

Ms. Dixon: You see, then I wasn't well. That was before I had this throat operation. Now I've had enough operations to make me feel healthier.

LILLIAN AND PETER FOGGO
CHILDREN: DANIEL, GAVIN

MR. FOGGO: Architect

Mr. Foggo: We would certainly not regard ourselves as formal. I'm using the word in its purest sense, in the sense that this house is formal because it has a conscious form. And our lifestyle we think is informal because it doesn't have a conscious form. But it may well be by American standards we are considered to be formal. In the sense that we tend to make up our lives as we go along, or at least think we do, and our habits are our own personal habits, our lifestyle is ours, we're not trying to emulate anybody else—in that sense we are informal. Not that we are rushing around madly trying to be informal or untraditional. That would be a form of formalism in one sense.

I am an architect. I was lucky that I just happened to drop into the one thing that I really wanted to do. I absolutely would not change my job for anything. I was born and brought up in Liverpool. My father had had a very insecure life, as the whole of that generation did—through the slums and whatever—and it was a reaction to that sort of life that made him and his generation want to put our generation into safe jobs—you know, with security and pensions and so on. And naturally the last thing I wanted was security.

I was about nine when the war broke out and was evacuated to mid-Wales eventually. And I spent nearly three years there on a farm. I got used to the country life and wanted to be a farmer. Anyway, when the bombing tailed off I returned to Liverpool and went to school with the aim of being a farmer. When I was fifteen I got fed up with school and left. I was put by my father into the bank, which I hated. You had to wear a tie, and it had to be a certain color, and you weren't allowed to take your jacket off, and on Saturday it was compulsory to wear a sports jacket. I mean that was compulsory to be gay on Saturday mornings! And I was fantastically miserable. In fact, I thought being miserable was a part of my personality.

Then I spent a lot of effort trying to get out of the

ABOUT THE PHOTOGRAPHS:

Mrs. Foggo: I think I prefer the outdoor photograph. Although it's posed, it's more informal than the other one.

Mr. Foggo: The indoor photograph is a very unnatural thing for us.

Mrs. Foggo: I don't know that just looking at one picture you can get an idea of what a family is like, apart from the size of it.

Mr. Foggo: For the same reasons that I don't like hearing my voice, I can't bear seeing my face on photograph. I just don't like the look of that face. I stare from behind it, so I don't see it. I'm very impressed with myself from behind my eyes, but I can't bear the physical manifestation at all.

bank, and eventually the only way out was to go into the army. I hated the army even more. About six months after leaving the army I sat in the middle of Liverpool one day, outside an architect's office, wondering what to do. I had no idea what architects did, but I was literally stimulated by the name of the firm on the wall. Within a week I was working in an architect's office, not as an architect but as an office boy. I gradually worked myself in, started going to night school and then eventually managed to get some money and went to university.

I remember walking into this architect's office for the first time and being absolutely overwhelmed just because they had their jackets off and were working in their shirt-sleeves. Anyway, that has nothing to do with my being an architect. Except it's an image thing for me.

ABOUT THE CHILDREN:
We try not to have any ambitions for our children. But it would be nice if they found something they enjoy doing. We wouldn't want to persuade them to be a doctor or whatever—that's the lesson we learned from my family. On the other hand, I think they could be helped to find it by exposing them, alerting their minds. I would like them to go to university. I think that's important, not because they learn to do anything there, but because in my life it was a fabulous way of meeting a vast cross-section of people and being exposed to fantastically widened horizons.

Mrs. Foggo: My father died just before I was two years old, and so I grew up with my sister and my mother—an all-female household. Though we were conscious of the war, we were pretty happy—very happy, in fact. We lived at a shop, a small grocer's shop, which my mother kept that was in the North of England, in Preston. I think my mother never had any views on education. It was my sister who went to university before me and took a French degree. I don't know where she got the idea. It must have been school, I suppose. It was just an assumption that I would go on to university as well. Well, I went to university in Liverpool, and I met Peter just as he was finishing his course. I took a degree in French. Then I worked until Gavin was born, doing research work for the Foreign Office. Well, of course, being a mother of two is a job. It has its satisfactory moments and its unsatisfactory moments. Now that both of them are at school, I am beginning to look around to see what I can do with myself which fits in with still having children around—you know, after school and at holidays. And I haven't resolved it yet. I am working on it. Because I have never had any idea about what I would like to do with my life, I very much envy people like Peter who have got this one thing in life that is satisfying. I would hope that my children could have the same kind of satisfying job that they would really enjoy doing.

ROSE AND JAMES HOMANS
CHILD: JESSIE
GRANDCHILDREN: LINDA, JOHN

MR. HOMANS: Railway worker

(Mr. Homans not photographed)

Mrs. Homans: We've been here in Pimlico nearly five years now. I don't like it here. I'd rather be back at Paddington where I used to live, where I lost me mother. You know why? 'Cause I was born in Paddington, I lived there all my life until I got married. My mom and daddy lived there before they died. And all their family lived there. No, I wish I never come here. I wish I was still in my mother's house.

I stick to myself. Well, I think it's the best way, you know. If you keep to yourself they can't say you said this, you said that.

My hubby said he wish he can get a place, a better place, you know, with a garden. You know, so he can get chickens and rabbits and that. You can't have no dogs or nothing in these council flats.

I'm in charge of my grandchildren. See, Linda don't call Jessie *Mother*, she calls me *Mother* and she calls my husband *Daddy*. We took right over. We took them over with our name. Jessie's going to go in hospital any time, see. That's why they let me properly in charge of Johnny and Linda. I keep them clean, go to school, bring them home, do their washing for them. I think of them as my own. Jessie has a handicap, you know. And that's why we're going to try and get her away in a hospital. So she can learn things, you know, sewing and that—like a training. I had one little girl. She died at six months of pneumonia. Then I had twins. They both died, you know, miscarriage. Then I had a mis and then I had Jessie.

THREE WISHES:

I wish I could get out of here, you know, get a flat with a garden for the children. Me own place. And I wish I could see my mother again. She was eighty-three when she died. And, well, I wish I could have another baby.

Mr. Homans: I detest this country. The Labour party, the Conservative, the Tories, they don't know what they want. Not only that. During the war when we come out of the army, now Churchill was a Conservative. Now he said while we was overseas, "the British soldier will come back to a better living accommodation." But we never did. We come back worse. I was out of the army four months. I married my wife. That was in October 1946. It took me thirteen years to get a council flat. That's after going in the army for six and a half years.

This country went too soft. They're too easy against immigrants. Even the people living in England, born and bred, they can't get housing.

So why should these immigrants get on before? These Asians come over here, they're over here about eighteen months, they own their own houses. They're over here a little while and they start putting in for tax. And their wives and children ain't here. They're back home. That's what I don't like.

There's lots of things. Look at the price of your food, the price of your coal, the price of the electric, your gas. It's all gone up. Since they joined that Common Market, this country's worse off. It's not only me. It's thousands of people that'll tell you that. We're worse off.

I work for the railway, doing messages and cleaning. It's all right. It's easy. But there's no money attached to it. Best thing, I travel free on the trains, I can take all my family for the price of one ticket. And I can go all over. It's a nice little job actually. It's a lovely job. There's no work attached to it.

My cough? That was through asphalt, sulphur fumes. You can never get rid of bronchitis. It runs in me family. Me father had it, I got it—Bill, Albert, Ronnie, one sister had it. That's five out of thirteen that's got it. My dad was working in the same asphalt firm all his life—since he come out of the 1918 war right up till he died about fourteen years ago.

I like one kind of thing that starts on the sixteenth of June. My wife, my daughter, two grandchildren and I go camping. That's what I like. And wrestling. Wrestling on the telly. Don't go to the pictures. And I like me beer. Nothing else. I got no interest in anything else. I got no interest in politics because none of them are any good. No matter who gets in.

When I come out of the army I was a right Communist. I'll tell you that. If the Communists was in, they wouldn't have all this nonsense. Look at Russia. They don't have all this nonsense, it's like France, they don't mess about. We was out in Malaya while the war was on, and the Communists and the guerrillas done more fighting against the Japs than what the load of us done. And when I come out in May 1946, two months later, this country sent British troops out there to round the Communist party up. And that's when I went Communist, because they done more fighting.

When I get of age, after sixty-five, I'll be going out topping, if you know what I mean. It's going out with a horse and cart and collecting like scrap iron, rags, cardboard. There's one place over in Kensington. They let you have a horse and cart out for thirty bob a week. But you got to buy all the food. Some weeks you might not get nothing. Another week you might earn twenty or thirty pound.

THREE WISHES:
I keep on telling her. If I ever come up on the pools I'd just walk out of here. I have a brother in Australia. He's better off. He's his own governor now. His missus is a dressmaker, and he's opened a free house, you know, sell any kind of beer. I've not seen him since 1948. So my wish is to win a load of money so I can go and see my brother out in Australia.

ABOUT THE PHOTOGRAPH:
Mr. Homans: No, I will not have me photo done. I will tell you why. Now since I come out of the army now I've had me photo done once with my people. And it seems I'm superstitious against it. Because since I had me three brothers and my father done together, it seems we all broke up and we're all gone a different way. If anybody goes to take a photo of me, I turn me back, because I don't like it.

Mrs. Homans: I would like a photo of my husband. I'd put it in a frame. Know what I mean? But he's afraid he might break the camera. He do!

PAULINE AND EDWARD ROHAN
CHILDREN: HELEN, EDWARD

MRS. ROHAN: Part-time secretary
MR. ROHAN: Constructural engineer

(Mr. Rohan not interviewed)

Mrs. Rohan: I have been in Pimlico for fifteen years. Before I was in the North of England, in Manchester. Just an average family. My dad was an electrician, and my mom used to do part-time jobs now and again to supplement the income. I was seventeen—I'd left school at sixteen—and I wanted to see the bright lights of London. My mother wasn't very happy about it, so she wrote off—I can't remember—to somebody saying did they have any jobs to offer. I could type and do a little bit of shorthand but nothing fantastic. And she got me a job in a hotel, as a receptionist in Victoria. And then I was lucky because the lady in charge was a very motherly type of person. You couldn't be in the hotel after twelve midnight, and that sort of stopped London from going to my head. You know, she used to always look after us. She was a wonderful person.

My husband Eddie comes from Ireland, one of sixteen children. They had a big farm, quite nice, and his father always wanted Eddie to run the farm. But the farm life wasn't for my husband. He always had a business head on him. He wanted the bright lights as well. He run away actually when he was sixteen—to London. After about three or four months he went to a technical college in Ealing, and then he got City and Guilds and little bits of certificates. I'm not very familiar with what it was. Now he's a constructural engineer and he's very pleased. He reads drawings and estimates things. He knew what he wanted. And he loves London. I think if I had the choice I would go back to the North of England. Because I've seen what London's all about and as far as my children were concerned, I think they'd get a much better education where I came from, you know, than what they're doing in London. It's much better for the children and it's a slower way of life. When you're down here, each year seems to go by like a month, because nobody's got time to stop and think about life any more. It's a rat race, and I don't want to feel I'm caught in it. I'd like to move to the country. We all got our utopia. I just want a simple life. Money doesn't mean very much to me. Money is an evil necessity. But I guess you've got to accept what you've got, really, haven't you? It's no use wanting things you can't have.

It's a very difficult period familywise. Eddie's a businessman at heart and he is determined to succeed. So the family, as such, has got to take second place. We don't do lots of things together, but we always do go on holidays together. Like last year we went to Jersey. Oh, it was beautiful. You know, lovely beach. Lovely, quiet, and peaceful. Our neighbors go everywhere together, and they're my ideal family unit. You know, they go to Mass together and they always seem to be going out as a family. When I was a child my dad always was going out walking with us and that was nice.

Well, I do go to church and the children do. My husband doesn't. He's a nonpracticing Catholic. Of the two of us, strangely enough, he's more religious. 'Cause when my little girl made her first Holy Communion, I was saying, "Is that dress all right?" Eddie said, "You've only got to please one person—up there." He wasn't bothered about how she looked as long as she was doing it for God.

ABOUT THE PHOTOGRAPH:

Mrs. Rohan: Well, the children don't look very much at ease on it. Helen, because she lost her front teeth, is looking very peculiar. I don't know why she was embarrassed about it. And Edward, you see how he's got his feet. He's usually very relaxed. But it looks like us. The photograph on the wall? We had that taken a year previous to you taking this one. Because I like family photographs. I think photographs are priceless in years to come. I mean, God forbid something happens, or even if it doesn't, it still would be nice to look back and see us all together. But I do love photographs. You know, they give a home the feeling of being home. There's a great big caseful upstairs.

DIANA AND ROBERT MORRIS
CHILDREN: SARA, EMILY

DR. MORRIS: Physician

Dr. Morris: As a medical student I lived in this area. And later, when I became a general practitioner, we decided we wanted to live in London. I had always had a dream about living in the country. We went and looked at various practices out in the country, and we decided that it was really rather dull. It hadn't got a lot of the things that were very important, like exhibitions, theater, and concerts. Not, of course, that we go to these things all the time every week. But we do go a lot.

I grew up in a suburb. Very standard middle-class public-school upbringing, minor public-school upbringing. I didn't want to be a doctor until about a year before I actually started to train. Before that I always wanted to do archaeology. The classic story is that I was told it didn't pay enough and my father's a doctor, so I decided I'd be a doctor.

Mrs. Morris: Like my husband, I grew up in the outer London suburbs. I always used to think it was rather an unexciting life. My stepfather used to work, and my mother just used to look after the house, and they used to garden at weekends and sometimes have tennis parties. That was the biggest excitement—having a tennis party in the garden on Sundays. I didn't like playing tennis and had to be made to play. I wanted something a bit more than that.

I lived in London since I was nineteen and have always wanted to stay here. I happened to go into nursing because it was quite a reasonable sort of life and you were occupied and you could live in London away from home. I also thought that I was never going to get married and that nursing was quite a good occupation for a spinster. I worked for six years as a nurse. No, I don't think I'll go back to it because it's really quite unsuitable for married people to nurse, especially in London, because I couldn't choose my hours. I think that running a home is much more satisfying and interesting than charging off to a hospital, really, and doing menial work that one could only do as a part-time person.

ABOUT THE CHILDREN:
Dr. Morris: I don't think I would ever send my children willingly to a boarding school. My reasons are partly political, partly I don't like the class system that goes into it, and partly because I think that the sort of state education one gets, particularly in London, is so much better now.

Mrs. Morris: There are two things really. One is that I'd like them to realize their potential, and we'll do everything in our power to help them realize that. And also I think I'd like them to be considerate—considerate of other people.

Question: Are you a typical English family, whatever that means?

Dr. Morris: A typical English family would be living in an outer London suburb.

Mrs. Morris: Or the suburbs of some other town, Manchester or Birmingham.

Dr. Morris: And a father that didn't have to work at weekends. And less money perhaps.

Mrs. Morris: I think of somebody in the country with a grand piano and daffodils . . . with a horse.

Dr. Morris: That's a literary view, though.

ABOUT THE PHOTOGRAPH:
Dr. Morris: It's quite a happy picture.

Mrs. Morris: Yes, the children looking slightly shy and nervous, which I think they probably are. My husband's looking rather suntanned and healthy.

Dr. Morris: Yes, we'd just come back from France.

Question: What are your views about the plain background?

Mrs. Morris: How could one choose just one picture for the background that would have been representative?

Dr. Morris: Yes. Much better to have nothing at all and let people accept us for what we are at that.

MARY SMITH
CHILDREN: SARA, ROSEMARY, CHRISTOPHER, MICHAEL, SUSAN, JOAN, JOHN

Mrs. Smith: I was brought up on a farm in Ireland. Before we went to school in the morning, we had to milk two cows each and get them water, you know, feed the hens and the pigs and all that. And then we had the same in the evening when we come in again. It wasn't easy. It was hard, considering nowadays what children get away with. We had no running water like we have here running out of the taps. I've got three sisters and one brother. They're all in Ireland apart from me.

I left when I was sixteen. I was a waitress in Ireland and I was only getting a pound a week and I thought I could do better if I came over here, which I did. I got eight pounds in London. Well, when I came I was all lost and I was all on me own, because I didn't know anybody over here. I wanted to go back home, but I stayed. But once I got settled in and had got a job, and you know, I made friends and that at work, I liked it over here. And I wouldn't go back to Ireland. I'd like to go home, you know, to see me mom and dad. I haven't been since John was two months and he's fourteen now, so that's about fourteen years now. I wouldn't go back there to live but I'd like to go back on a holiday if I could afford to take the children with me.

My husband died in June, seven years ago this June. And I found I had quite a few friends here when he died, when I needed them most. Because my oldest was only seven and my youngest was twelve months and I was six weeks pregnant for Sarah. I had no relations here and no mother and no father or anybody, and I found that friends did help in. It was hard. When my husband was alive, even though there was fourteen or fifteen months between a lot of my children, I never found it hard, and you know, it never got on top of me. Because he was always there to help me.

I try to do the best I can. I kept the children all together. I've always been independent as well. I'd help other people and I'd look after other people's children, but I would never ask anybody to help me or to look after my children. Wherever I went, the children come too. People said to me, "Mary, you can leave your children with me." "You can go out." But I said no, I didn't want to go out and leave the kids. Not that I didn't trust them. I did trust them. But I've always been like that, ever since they were babies. The only place they didn't come was down to the graveyard when my husband died. I was going to take them with me and my friends said no, that wasn't the place for them.

I know I won't get married again. I know that for sure. I wouldn't get married now because I wouldn't want the children to have a stepfather, although a lot of people have turned around and said they need a father. But I don't think so. Because I've been father and mother to them for nearly seven years. So I don't see how they need one now. I'm very strict and always have been. But I wouldn't let anybody hit them. If anybody hit them, I think I'd kill him. I'm quite happy the way I am, and they're happy the way they are. They don't want for anything.

THREE WISHES:
That I'd win the pools and take the children to see me mom in Ireland, 'cause she's never seen them. She's longing to see them.

ABOUT THE PHOTOGRAPH:
I don't know. They all look like they're going to be shot. I had an operation then, didn't I? Everybody says I look much better now. And I put on weight since then as well. For five years I was in and out of hospital, for thrombosis. Sometimes I wasn't even out for three months and I was back in again. Oh, I've done very well now.

JACKIE AND MICHAEL GLAVIN
CHILD: WILLIAM

MRS. GLAVIN: Part-time office cleaner
MR. GLAVIN: Electrician

(Mr. Glavin not interviewed)

Mrs. Glavin: I've lived more or less around this area all my life. I was born in Chelsea. I love it. I'd never move out. I just wish maybe the flats we live in could be just a bit more livable, if you know what I mean. They're too small, too compact, not enough room for the children and all this. But it's what you make of it. My parents are both Irish. I've been over to Ireland quite a few times. I think an awful lot of Ireland. I wouldn't hear nothing said against the Irish. I mean there's good and bad in every race as far as I'm concerned, and that's it.

My father worked all over the place actually. He used to work on the papers, on the print, and then he worked on the railways and my mother, you know, she doesn't work now but when she did, she was a cook.

I had a strict upbringing. When everyone else was going to a dance and had to be home at twelve, we had to be home at ten. I used to say, "Oh, it's not fair! When I grow older I'm going to do this and I'm going to do that." But I never did. And now when I look back on it, I'm glad my parents were like that, because who knows where I'd be now if they weren't.

I want to give William the best. If he's got the brains, well and good, I'd like him to get on and get himself a good job, get on, you know, and have something behind him. But if he hasn't, then fair enough, let him go in for a trade or an apprenticeship or something. Whatever he wants to do, you know, it suits me, as long as he's happy and he knows this is home—he can come back when he wants to. I was never forced to do anything, so I wouldn't force my child to do it either.

THREE WISHES:
I'd like to have money, you know. I'd love to have money. I'd like to have a beautiful family, which I've got now anyway, but I'd like everything to be all right if I had any more children. I'd just hope they'd be all right. And I'd like to live to a nice old age to see them all get on in life as well as what I hoped. That's it really.

ABOUT THE PHOTOGRAPH:
Mrs. Glavin: It's not a very nice background, but then again it can't be helped. It's where we live. But, you know, the actual photograph, I think it's a good likeness of all of us. The best I've ever had taken of me 'cause I'm not a bit photogenic. William's got a bit bigger since then, and he's filled out an awful lot more. So have I! Yes, I think it's good.

MARY AND DENNIS DOWNES

MR. DOWNES: Retired decorator

Mr. Downes: This country I love very much. I come from Ireland, and you never deny your nationality, if you know what I mean, but in myself I feel I am a Londoner, you know, because I mix so much with the London people. I love it. And I'm proud of my children, and that I brought them up in this country.

We know it's troublesome times. I mean the price of food and everything else is going up now and rents and the phones.

Mrs. Downes: The social security people are very good, you know. He gets insurance sickness benefit and the social security benefit. But if you want a day's outing, they don't give you much room. The only thing you can do is on the buses. We've got free tickets to go on the buses.

Mr. Downes: I used to work for Westminster City Council, interior decoration, you know. Then I got ill and had to be retired from work. When I was working we used to go here and there and get what we wanted. Now you can't. You got to just sit in there and wait for something to blow in. I'm not a pensioner. My wife is, but she won't get her pension when I come of age. You see, I am six years younger.

Mrs. Downes: I come over here in 1936 from County Tipperary, the South of Ireland. I had all the family over here. That's why I come over here. Because we lost our parents when we were very young. And I come here to look after the brothers and sisters.

When we were married, we went to the council and they were very good to us. We've never been without a home since we've been under the council. Oh, I wouldn't live anywhere else. It's sociable and you've got everything near you. We live on the twelfth floor and it's smashing.

Mr. Downes: I love it up here.

Mrs. Downes: The people in the building mostly keep all to theirselves, you know. You never know if they're ill or anything. They don't come and tell you they're ill, and you don't know until you miss them going in and out.

We go to the Red Cross. It's very sociable there. You meet nice persons there. You know, you can play cards or sit down and read and play bingo. Small things like that. It's very good over in the Red Cross. And we go to the daughter's now and then, and we do babysitting for them.

I was working right up to the time they retired my husband through his illness. And I retired to look after him, be home with him, you know. Otherwise I'd still be working. My favorite job was always in restaurants, cooking and dishing up dinners and that. And I used to like cashier work as well. You know you miss the company of working and that.

THREE WISHES:

Mr. Downes: I wish I could win the premium bonds. I'd like to go to the United States. I really would. I have one sister in America, Mary, my eldest sister. But I never hear from them. They don't know if I'm dead or alive really. I'd like to see the President of the United States, Mr. Nixon. I think he's a lovely bloke. This Watergate business. There has been a lot of bribery in the White House, years ago. But President Nixon today, I don't think he's that type of person. He hasn't got that look, if you know what I mean. He has a very pleasant look. I like the man very much, and you can tell them back in the United States that I told you that too. I stand by him every day.

Mrs. Downes: Well, my wishes would be to go back home to Ireland for a good rest, a good holiday at home.

ABOUT THE PHOTOGRAPH:

Mrs. Downes: This one is exactly how we are now, isn't it?

Mr. Downes: People who'd look at the photograph, they'd say, "Well, Mr. Downes, you've lost some weight." That's all. But this is how I look, as I am now.

DOROTHY AND JOHN CHARGE
CHILDREN: DANIEL, STEPHEN, PATRICIA, LESLIE, DAVID, ROSEMARY

MR. CHARGE: Dustman

Mrs. Charge: I'm a right Londoner. I was born by Covent Garden market, Trafalgar Square, Leicester Square. You know, right there where on a quiet day they reckon you can hear the sound of Bow Bells. And if you're born within the sound of Bow Bells, then you're supposed to be a Cockney. That was the thing. I never listened!

I was six when the war started and we were evacuated, first to Reading, then to Hungerford, where we spent a couple of years. Then we were in such a dilapidated state of health my mom brought us home, around the time when you had all the blitz and the incendiary bombs. Then the flying bombs and the doodlebugs, and then when the rockets started coming over my dad made us go away again. And we went away for about a year and the war ended.

But the war was a happy time. People helped each other. Made a cup of tea, everybody had a cup of tea. You had the old piano going. Everybody came in for a singsong.

Question: What is your idea of fun?

Mrs. Charge: There's a group of mothers here in Peabody, all with families, and we have a day out or certain nights out. And we go to the seaside for the day. This year we've been saving five shillings a week, and we're going to have an evening out at the Lyceum, down the Strand. You know, the old-time music hall. And we have a good knees-up and a good singsong, which we enjoy. Then there's a club we belong to which is a working man's club at Battersea, and you take all your family. They've got a bar where you can sing and another place where you can play darts. You get a lot of cabbies down there as well. And of course I like playing bingo.

ABOUT THE CHILDREN:
You can only teach them or show them. After that, all the experiences in the world that you had you can't really teach them anything. They can only learn by experience. If the child hasn't got it in him, nothing on God's earth will make him be that.

I think good manners and treating people as you'd like to be treated yourself is important. Oh, one thing. The littlest one, Danny, he's a fanatic footballer, and he has been from the day he was born. And I'd love to be there one day at Wembley in about twenty years' time or less. When he'll be playing for England. We'll all be sitting at Wembley and they'll all be singing "Danny Boy." That I would like to see.

Mr. Charge: I used to work for the railway and packed that up. Then my brother-in-law, he worked on the council, and he got me a job there. I collect anything anybody wants taken away, what the regular dustmen won't take, tables and things. It's called *trade collectors.* Dustmen only travel on certain streets, and we travel all over Westminster.

It's all right. You know, you see more of life than you do in an ordinary office or something like that. You see something different every day. Oh, it's hard work. You can do twelve ton a day, easy. Some days it's lighter. It depends on what people throw out. Things got better since the strike, but not as good as, I mean, a man in a factory. It's a strong union, but the point is, all governments are the hardest ones to get any money out of. But now that the job's got better, the turnover is just over retirement or death sort of thing, you know. Otherwise people will stay 'cause it's a secure job, you see.

ABOUT THE PHOTOGRAPH:

Mrs. Charge: Well, strangers would never believe John was a Londoner for a start. Not John. He looks Italian, really. It would have been better if you had caught everybody sitting doing something, rather than standing in a group. It wouldn't look so artificial.

Mr. Charge: There's two kids missing on it, so it's not the full family, is it?

ELIZABETH AND RON ROOTES
CHILD: AMANDA

MR. ROOTES: Pub manager

Mr. Rootes: You know those huge car people, the Rootes? We are directly related to them by my grandfather. We were meant to be rich. Do you realize that? My grandfather fell in love with the cook in the household. They said, "If you marry her, you'll be banished from the family." Well, he married her, and they slept in the stable. They had twenty-four children. My dad's one of the youngest and he's sixty, you see.

My father is a painter and decorator. A really good craftsman. I spent my first sixteen years in England, just outside London. All my schooling was here. I went to New Zealand for a working holiday and never really came back except to visit. All my family is there now. Liz and I came back to England two and a half years ago, but we aren't going to stay. I think the world of England. You know, New Zealanders refer to England as home.

Mrs. Rootes: In New Zealand all the nurses in my class, just about ninety-nine percent of them, came to England for a trip when they finished. That was the thing to do.

Mr. Rootes: You see, it's a matter of money. If I had fifty thousand pounds I'd never leave England.

Mrs. Rootes: We can live so much better over there, can't we? And here we don't have a garden or anything.

Mr. Rootes: It's not that. You can have a garden here. But there's no room for advancement in England. We're doing all right here, but the effort I put into this place, for the same thing in New Zealand I could be much better off.

Mrs. Rootes: We're going back to New Zealand next year.

Mr. Rootes: The chances are that Amanda will go to university in New Zealand, even with an average intelligence. I mean I would have gone to university if I had been there. In England I was in the top of my class all the way through, but I got eliminated. In New Zealand even the dummies are looked after.

I'd love to stay here, but how could we live if we didn't live in the pub? We couldn't even get a flat. In New Zealand I will have a licensed restaurant. And I can say definitely, "We're going to have a restaurant," whereas in England I could say, "Well, we *might* have a restaurant, if we're lucky." And I can also say that in New Zealand, "We'll have a house."

Question: How is it running a pub?

Mrs. Rootes: It's really fun. Ron and I get on very very well together, which you've got to do anyway. Quite a few couples break up running a pub because you're together twenty-four hours a day. I do the cooking and the book work and Ron does everything else.

Mr. Rootes: It's seven days a week, but we've got it nicely organized. You're respected and it's nice. Like when you're host of the party everyone respects you because they're at your place. It's up to you whether the atmosphere is happy because it goes from the staff to the customers.

Mrs. Rootes: There's a happy-go-lucky atmosphere here because we get on socially with most of the staff. You know, we have a really good time.

Mr. Rootes: I don't stomp around in a suit and all that. I feel just like everyone else in the place except that I know that my name is over the door and I'm responsible. You know, there's no such thing as class distinction in New Zealand. So when you come back to England you can't swallow it. It just seems so false.

ABOUT THE PHOTOGRAPH:

Mr. Rootes: The photograph looks Victorian. And I never look like I think I look.

Mrs. Rootes: We look like that when we're going out—to a certain party or a meeting. The rest of the time we wear jeans. Amanda's dress? I think it's about a hundred and something years old. I wore it, my brother wore it, mummy wore it, grandfather wore it and great-grandfather wore it. We actually had her christened in it, you know.

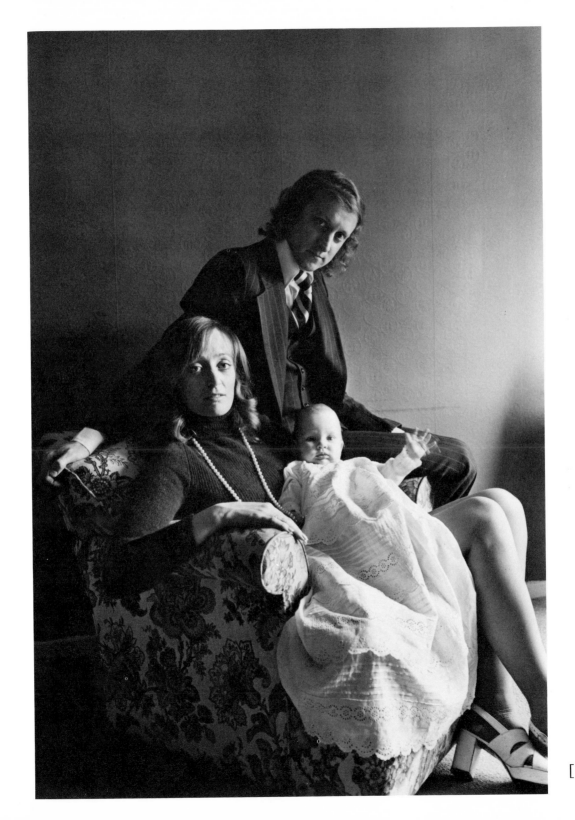

BOO AND BILL ANDREWS
CHILDREN: ALEXANDER, EDWARD, SOPHIE
DOG: MATILDA

MR. ANDREWS: Businessman

Mr. Andrews: From age six I was really brought up in parts of the country in Worcestershire. And I came to London to work because it is where the action is. I like living here five days a week, provided that I can get away on the weekend. I'd be miserable living here seven days a week, and in fact wouldn't do it. I would change my job and reorganize my life to be able to be in the country.

I don't think we really consider ourselves Londoners, although we probably are in truth. We've come to live fairly much a London life, but I think the country element in it plays a very strong part. In a sense where you live when you're working is almost less important than what you do at the weekend. There's no doubt, having five days in London with all its theaters and tremendous number of people and a lot of things going on, and two days in the country, is a very very pleasant experience. And we never take it for granted. We are very very lucky.

I've always been in business. Now I run a small public company, a small leisure group running discothèques, casinos, amusement arcades, that kind of popular entertainments. My work has always been very important to me—the organizing and the motivating of people, taking a view of what they want and trying to provide it. But the particular line of business is less important to me. This is where I happen to be at the moment, but it's not necessarily where I'll be forever.

Mrs. Andrews: I lived in Scotland, in the North of Scotland, Aberdeenshire, miles away from anywhere. I think I had a very lovely childhood in the wilds of Scotland. My mother's American. My father was a landowner and a soldier. He was away a lot. It was the war. I went to school in England. I did a secretarial course and worked in London. Then I met Bill and got married. If I had

my way I'd go back to Scotland, all things being equal. But I like living in here. I think Pimlico's lovely. All the nice shops and the people. It really has got a cross-section of people. And all the children you see go to the same schools nearby. I think that helps mix people.

ABOUT THE CHILDREN:
Mr. Andrews: I would want them to do something really energetically, I suppose. It doesn't almost matter what. But I would like them to be keen enough on something to put a tremendous amount of energy and effort into it. I think the only thing that would really disappoint me would be if they didn't care about anything. That I would find very disappointing. And I think having some sort of personal integrity is important, so that if you say you'll do a thing you'll do it.

Question: Don't you think that your ideas on "energy" are not typically English?

Mr. Andrews: Yes. I think one of the biggest problems in this country is a slight sneering at energy. It's smarter to be not particularly energetic. To be rather sophisticated about everything, you know.

Mrs. Andrews: It's changing a bit, I would say. I mean, gone are the days of smart lounging about.

Mr. Andrews: Yes. This business of energy is important. That you are prepared to have a go at something and put a lot of time and effort into it.

THREE WISHES:
Mr. Andrews: Probably the things I would wish for would be slightly frivolous things in that it would be very very nice to buy or breed a really good hunter which turned out to be an absolutely super horse. I'd love to do that. But I think when one's lucky enough to have things like one's health and children and happiness, one hesitates to think about magical wishes. It seems so greedy to wish for anything more.

Mrs. Andrews: I always wish that I'll die first. That would be my wish.

MARSHA HUNTE
CHILD: SIMON

I was born in Hereford on the border of Wales, in the country, and I came down to London when I was five. And I've lived here ever since and I wouldn't change it. My dad grew up in Trinidad. He came to London when he was twenty-one, and he's been here ever since. He's a cabdriver. My mother was born in Kentish Town. She was a secretary until she took ill with arthritis. I always go around and see my parents. They're still very happy together.

I had quite a strict upbringing myself, although it didn't do me any good. As for going out and everything, we wasn't allowed to go many places, not like the majority of teenagers my age. They used to go to clubs and everything. I think a lot of colored people are like that, you know; they're very strict with their children, I find.

I want Simon to be a good sort of man when he grows up. I don't expect nothing exceptional for him, but if he does, all well and good. He never causes me any trouble and I hope he doesn't in the future. I hope he just stays on the right track.

When I was at home I was very quiet, completely different, but now that I have a place of my own I've had to be very independent. And I've grown up a lot more, I think, as well. Now I sort of speak my mind and say what I have to say. Some of the old people around here used to pick on me a lot when I first moved in here, and I don't know if that is because I didn't have a husband. But I won't stand for it. I mean, I'm not rude to people. If they talk to me properly I talk to them back. But I won't let people order me about, because I don't find that is right no matter who the person is.

I hope to be able to move out of these buildings within the next few years. I just hope I can get something better in the future—more space and a better flat as well. I am not used to flats with bathrooms in the kitchens.

THREE WISHES:
I'd love to have a house of my own. In London, sort of just on the outskirts of London, not too far out. I'm getting married this year and I just hope everything works out all right. And I would like to take my son with me around the world and show him a few different countries. I just hope one day I shall be able to do it.

ABOUT THE PHOTOGRAPH:
Simon looks spotless there, but it's only because he was having his photo done. And it does me justice, actually. I think it's very natural.

ELIZABETH AND ANDREW TROTTER
CHILD: SARAH

MR. TROTTER: Policeman

Mr. Trotter: I think I was a reasonable, mature child. I had no fantastic dreams about adult life. I had no great expectations. Life is what you make it.

I came to London to join the police force. I wanted a job that got me into the open. I didn't fancy an office job at all. And I didn't want to be able to predict whatever I would be doing every day. My job is the way I make my living. It's the way I keep my family and my means of obtaining accommodation. I'm fond of my job. It's a good job and I don't think I could ever leave it really. But I don't take it too seriously.

We do the job we are paid for. We don't necessarily have to believe entirely in the laws we are upholding. We're not on a crusade. We are ordinary workers and we're doing an ordinary job.

My two brothers are in the police force. My father had spent some time in it too. For a while, I was rather anti joining the police force and very stuck on agriculture. But working as a farm manager is working purely for someone else's profit and not my own. So my interest in that side faded.

I am leaving London to get away into the countryside and to get my daughter away from central London—to get a back garden for her and prospects for a better education out in the country. I would not consider bringing up a child in central London.

I would certainly like to buy my own house. This is still my main priority in life, so that I have more independence from my job.

One of the present sicknesses in London is that people who provide the service industries of London are having to move further and further from London, purely because they can't afford to live here. This is why so many police-men are leaving London; they can't afford to buy property here.

ABOUT THE CHILD:
I would like our children to go as far as possible in their education, to go to university and to take the time to decide what to do with their lives.

Question: Can you put yourselves in a class?

As far as my wages go, I would put myself definitely in the working class. I think I would put myself from my background and education into the middle class, I would say.

Mrs. Trotter: My husband deals mainly with his work and I mainly have a say in the home. We discuss everything. My job is basically looking after my family, keeping them as happy and contented as possible. That is my main purpose and that is what I want to do. I would work if I had to. But I think the woman's place is in the home. It's very rewarding to bring up a family. If you look after your own little piece and everybody looks after theirs, I think the world would be a happier place.

For the baby, I want happiness for herself. The only material thing I want is our own home because that is security.

I also think security is a stable background, which is what I think I've had and what I think is most important for the children throughout their lives. A stable, home-loving background.

I was always interested in nursing, looking after children, which has come out in my own child. My parents were not ambitious for me. They wanted me to have a good grounding secretarial course. For my children I want them to do what they want to do and be happy doing it. That's all there is.

ABOUT THE PHOTOGRAPH:
Mr. Trotter: I like the photograph of myself in uniform. I think it isn't stilted. It is rather jolly, as we normally are.

DOREEN AND ALBERT SNOOKS
CHILDREN: PAUL, RYAN

MR. SNOOKS: Caretaker

(Mrs. Snooks not interviewed)

Mr. Snooks: Actually, they're really taking part of London away, you know, by building more flats. How can I say it? The houses that are here now, they're taking them down. I mean, some people like it, some people don't. I'm one who would rather keep London as London was, with all the houses in it. I mean, you haven't got the neighbors now. Before everyone could have a laugh and giggle where now people shut their door and you don't see them, till right the next day. Whereas when it was houses, you know, you always had someone on the door talking to one another. I feel sad because, how can I say it, we're getting more like Europe now. We've got one building over here now that's on the Embankment. It's twenty-two floors high. To me, they're really killing London by doing this.

I was born here in London. Actually, where I was born was Sloane Square, near St. Michael's. My father used to work on the railway. He didn't like the idea of housing coming down to put flats up.

I'm maintaining the flats I'm living in, like, you know, keeping them clean and helping the public out on any emergencies—mainly lifts and burst pipes and maybe the odd one or two tap washers. And mainly the elderly people, like, you know, they normally go out and forget their key and we've got to find a way of getting in for them, mainly through the windows half the time.

But it's not too bad. Up to a point it's interesting, like, you can meet people, like every day you meet someone new. I've got about five buildings to look after, but it's not too bad.

Before I got married I was working in a factory. But we couldn't get housing accommodation, and this was the only way of getting somewhere to live. Yeah, I get a rent-free flat here. And I don't think I would move from here,

'cause we get the guards coming down here every morning, you know, to go to Buckingham Palace. That goes by every morning and that's a nice sight to see.

Some people, you know, are going more Continental now. Like the Royal Family. Some are beginning to say, "Why do we need a figurehead now? We're in the Common Market now." Well, my view is that as long as I live I hope we have got a figurehead here. Like, someone where I can turn around and say, "Well, that's the King and Queen of England." It's terrific, you know, when people come over here and they say to you, "Can you tell me how to get to the Buckingham Palace?" I really feel proud of it, not only because I'm English but proud to tell them how to get there. I think if we didn't have a Queen, we wouldn't have people coming here.

My wife is a housewife, but when she's done her housework, when the boys are in bed, she'll probably sit down and normally, if I'm not here she'll have the records on, 'cause she is a record-lover.

Normally, if I'm here, we'll have a quiet night watching telly. Well, now and again we might get someone in to mind the babies and we'll go out, like have a night out. And normally we'll go to a local cinema, and come out of there and go and have a Wimpy, and come home.

Normally for our holidays we hire a caravan for a fortnight. Last year we was down in Kent. On these caravan sites you've got everything you want there, like a clubhouse, swings, and paddling pool for the youngsters to go into. You've got a dog's swimming pool there. And you don't have to worry about what you're going to do that day. Everything down there is organized.

The ambition I would like my children to do would be, you know, foreign travel a bit so they see how other countries live like. I wouldn't like them to get about eighteen and then go and get married. I'd like them to see a bit of the world first. I've been to Austria, Sweden, Switzerland, and France, but the countries I'd really like to go to is Canada, America, and I'd like to go to Russia. You know, I want to find out how these countries live.

MARGOT AND ANDREW SLATER
CHILDREN: BARNABY, KATE

MR. SLATER: Restaurant owner

Mr. Slater: I am a suburbaner by birth and a Londoner by inclination. We chose this area because it's easy to get to the places we wanted to go. And we knew the Pimlico tube station was coming along. We do go to the theater, now maybe seven or eight times a year. Before we had two children, probably twenty times a year. We also like the cinema. We go to a number of exhibitions, not as many as we intend to go to. A lot of our friends are in London, and those that aren't are scattered around London.

When I came to Pimlico I was sales promotion and advertising manager for the Shell retail division of Shellmex and B.P. I can claim some of the credit or accept some of the blame for the number of coins and glasses and steak knives which were distributed to motorists.

Then I thought, I have always wanted to work for myself, let's get out before I am forty, and what can I do. The first fourteen months I got more involved in property because it just happened to be that I stumbled upon a property boom . . . and then I saw that this boom was partly artificial, and some of the more unsavory aspects of the property world I found unattractive. And so, partly for self-interest and partly perhaps out of altruism—although self-interest came first—I thought, let's do my love rather than the purely economic, which is my new restaurant or rather restaurants. They are going to be Greek restaurants—informal, quite noisy, good food, not haute cuisine, medium-priced.

I would say I am not ambitious for the children, in that I don't particularly mind whether they make a lot of money or not. I would like to see them stretched to their ability.

We are not a typical English family. To give a facetious answer, I can't stand cricket for a start. I don't like going to pubs very much, I have never seen a professional football match, though I would like to see one, I like food better than the average Englishman, and I like foreigners better than the average Englishman.

THREE WISHES:
To start from the global end and work downwards. I would like to see the various sides involved in the Middle East problem getting down and sorting out somewhere for the Palestinians to live and something that would give the Israelis sufficient security. I would like to see a more united feeling about this country. Coming down to a personal level, my immediate wish is to see a successful restaurant. Work starts on Monday, and with a bit of luck . . .

Mrs. Slater: We came to Pimlico four years ago because we wanted a bigger house. We had lived in a tiny little house in Chelsea which we had bought, frankly, because we didn't think we were going to have any children. Suddenly, the marvelous thing happened and we had Katey. . . . In Pimlico you get a tremendous cross-section of people. For example, at Katey's dancing class, one sits and chats with all the mothers, and we all seem to share the same problems, although, let's face it, they are working-class mothers and I suppose I am not really. And this is how it should be.

I was in publicity. After I had Katey, I worked at home for eighteen months. And then my son arrived and that really put an end to my working.

Both children are very attractive children. They give us tremendous pleasure, and frankly, I love working in the house, looking after them. I really do. Now that Andrew is working at home, we are a very integrated family.

PATRICIA AND WILLIAM BORIOSI
DAUGHTER: PAMELA
GRANDSON: NICHOLAS

MR. BORIOSI: Wine waiter
PAMELA: Shoe saleswoman

Mr. Boriosi: I've been in London all my life. Both my father and mother came from Italy. Well, my father was in catering, you see. And like my son is a chef. And I am a wine waiter. I have been doing it for years. It's a club where I work now.

They're drinking a lot of wine here, yes. It's all wine now. I go into pubs, but I like to drink at home. I have my drink here. Rum, you know.

THREE WISHES:
I'd like to go and see America. I've got friends of mine working in America.

Mrs. Boriosi: I was born in Worcester, and I've lived in London twenty-eight years. I had a hard life in Worcester, because I've had two stepfathers and I was pushed about a lot. But my mother was very very kind and so was my aunts and uncles. But being born before marriage, they seem to have a lot against you. I don't know for why, but that seems to be what happens. And I was pushed into service and then I've made my own way up. I worked as an orderly in a hospital and I've got on from there. Then I met my husband and we married. I've enjoyed bringing the children up. I haven't had very much trouble with any of them. They're all good workers and they're all very pleasant and very thoughtful. And I've got a good husband. That's what makes the difference, I think, to life. I've got nothing to complain about, nothing at all.

THREE WISHES:
Well, good health for both of us, which I'm not enjoying at the moment very much, but otherwise to live like we have been living. My husband's very giving. If we want anything, he'll do his best to get it for us. He's very thoughtful.

ABOUT THE PHOTOGRAPH:

Mr. Boriosi: It's all right. I wasn't well when I had this photograph taken. I knew I was going into the hospital. I had an operation after that.

Mrs. Boriosi: His eyes look terrible there, don't they? I think the photo's good, very good indeed. I mean I look very big there, because it was a closeup, but I'm not really that big, am I?

Mr. Boriosi: The coat hanger's crooked . . . and it's still crooked now, isn't it?

ANN AND MICK MUNDY

CHILDREN: ANGELA, JAMES, SIMON

MR. MUNDY: Transport driver

Mrs. Mundy: Funnily enough, my family came from Chelsea, around about King's Road. I definitely do like living in London. When we first had the twins and Angela, all I wanted was to sort of get out and have a house and a garden.

Mr. Mundy: We have thought about moving to a new town, but it doesn't really appeal to us actually.

Mrs. Mundy: I had all the new town forms and papers and things. But we have this friend who moved to a new town. The more I went down to see her, the more I didn't want to live there. There's just nothing at all.

Mr. Mundy: In these new towns you're lucky if you've got a cinema. The other thing is the housing. All the houses are bleak, you see. And they look like rows and rows of chicken huts. The only good thing about all these places in fact is that they have a lot of green grass, which is fine.

Mrs. Mundy: And all these towns consist of young couples, say between twenty-five and thirty-five, with young children. So when this lot grows up, three won't be anybody.

Mr. Mundy: So, we'll stay in London, which in fact does have a lot going for it.

Mrs. Mundy: I don't think the kids really miss out on anything because they're living in London.

Mr. Mundy: We've been in Churchill Gardens Estate for about a year but we've not met a lot of people, surprisingly. I mean we know the neighbors and a few people on this block, but apart from that . . . I think, in fact, flats actually are killers, to be honest. When you live in a house you come out your front door and you know everyone that goes up and down that street, right, and you meet lots of people that way. In flats you walk in, you get in the lift, you come up to the second floor, bang, you're there. You don't meet anybody.

I drive a lorry for an air service. Well, I work from Heathrow Airport, just delivering and collecting air freight. I used to be an engineer, for about twelve years. I worked on machines, you know, on the lathes, milling. I was made redundant, actually. But I was getting a bit fed up with engineering anyway. All that lovely sunshine, and I was stuck inside grease and oil. So I thought I'd have a go at driving. I like my job. My idea of fun? I must admit I like a drink, although I don't go to the pub every day. But almost. And I like driving, even though I do it for a job. I'd like to have a nice car. You know, a nice Mercedes or something like that.

Mrs. Mundy: I enjoy going down to the pub to have a drink. We go down to the Fox in Pimlico. I like meeting people. And I go to the needlework class on a Tuesday, and I go to a mothers' discussion group on Thursday. It's a break away from the children, you know. But I must admit I do like having a drink and going out for a nice meal.

THREE WISHES:
Mrs. Mundy: I definitely would like to have a home in London, and I'd like to have a home in the country too. Definitely have somebody living in to do the cooking and the housework. I'd never have a nanny. The children would be mine. And I'd love to go to one of these health farms for about a month or two. I've got to lose about three stone, and it would take me two months to do that.

ABOUT THE PHOTOGRAPH:
Mrs. Mundy: I don't think that really shows us. I mean it looks as though I'm sort of standing there posed, all nice for the photograph, not interested in the kids at all. And Mick's down there with his arm around Angela, sort of much more natural than I.

Mr. Mundy: No, I disagree. No, I think in fact it portrays us pretty well. I think it's O.K.

Mrs. Mundy: The twins look so good there, don't they! So angelic and that. And they're not a bit like that, really.

ELAINE AND RALPH GOODMAN

MRS. GOODMAN: School teacher
MR. GOODMAN: Businessman

Mrs. Goodman: My father's English and my mother's Irish. Actually, I came from Northern Ireland about seven years ago. When I was at school and old enough to have a job, you might say seventeen, I used to go away at the summer holidays and the Easter holidays, and very often I came to London. Because I hated Northern Ireland. I never liked it and I don't think I ever will. I love the countryside, but I just don't like the people. . . . I'm narrow-minded and I'm bigoted, and I am very bad-tempered, and I think these are characteristics of the Northern Irish.

Mr. Goodman: I went abroad at six months old and spent all my life abroad—Africa, Asia. On one of my leaves, I looked for a flat in London. This was 1961. I found one in Pimlico and I bought it.

Moving back to England was a difficult adjustment. But if you're an expatriate, when you come back you appreciate living here more than the people do who've been living here all their lives.

Mrs. Goodman: Ralph has been writing poetry.

Mr. Goodman: A lot of poetry. I keep it in the attaché case. I shall revise it forever. I've always been a businessman. Poetry is a sideline.

Mrs. Goodman: I think maybe you should write some more poetry, honey.

Mr. Goodman: Yes, maybe I should. This has to do with living abroad. It's called "The Expatriate."

We are the expatriates.
Once upon a time we all came from good public schools.
Fearless fools, defiant, self-reliant,
Turned out by a sausage machine
To govern vast tracts of land for the Queen.
These days we are mostly cynical,
Coughing carpetbaggers selling machines
Or mending machines or collecting curved daggers.
Not so defiant, more pliant.

Gunboats have given way to the export drives
But we lead similar lives,
Drinking pink gins, forgiving black sins.
Leave looms large.
And when we come home you will see us cluster
In pubs, clubs, and Chinese restaurants,
Reminiscing proudly, but far too loudly,
Waving the flag of past parties, orgies, hangovers,
Why the raj was great, whose wife became whose mate,
Recalling the naval names on the inevitable crests
Upon the walls of the British Club, burnt in the latest riots.
Have you got your work permit?
We do not sunbathe in the squares or at the seaside.
Because we know the sun to be our enemy.
Our time of infinite patience lies inside
Washing our shirts is beyond us,
Cleaning of shoes is beneath us,
But packing of bags and weatherbeaten wives
To leave an alien land, the jungle or the sand
Is the curved dagger of our lives.

Mrs. Goodman: I think the awful thing is that Ralph hasn't written a poem in about three years.

Mr. Goodman: I'm too happy.

Mrs. Goodman: Ralph has it all worked out. We're going to buy a house in the countryside, and he's going to retire, and I am going to teach in a school nearby . . .

Mr. Goodman: . . . and keep me. We're going to retire to a village where they have good draft beer—which is unusual these days—where they have a nice school where Elaine can teach and keep me in the style to which I am accustomed. I'll drink my draft beer every day and write a little poem now and again. And you know, this is going to happen. That's the awful thing!

ABOUT THE PHOTOGRAPH:

Mr. Goodman: No, you can never get the right impression of people just by looking at a photograph. Strangers would think that we live in a bigger flat than we do. I mean, we live in a very pokey flat.

VICTORIA AND ANTONY HURST
CHILDREN: CHARLOTTE, MIRANDA

MR. HURST: Social work administrator

Mrs. Hurst: When I was living at home, I always wanted to live in the center of London in these mid-Victorian, early Victorian terraces, because I think they are so pretty and so historically interesting. "At home" was the suburbs which I didn't like very much.

Mr. Hurst: We bought this house about three months after we were married, about eight years ago, and we have lived here ever since. It's my idea of one extreme of where I want to live. There are obvious disadvantages of living in the middle of London.

Mrs. Hurst: Well, the disadvantages are that it's very short on green space, which affects the children, obviously. There's far too much traffic and it's too noisy. But it has tremendous advantages. It's exciting and it's full of people, and you can walk to the Tate Gallery, and after the theater you can walk home across the park. It means an awful lot to me to be living somewhere as historic as this, to be able to go by the Houses of Parliament almost every time you take a short bus ride. It's tremendously exciting.

Mr. Hurst: And we really do do these things. Well, we don't do them every day or every week, but the fact that we go to the Tate and do walk there is quite an important factor in our lives. I mean it's not just a pretend.

You ask about my background. I grew up half in Staffordshire and half in Hampshire. My two grandfathers provide the most splendid contrast with each other that you could possibly imagine. One is landed gentry who was knighted for services to the British Foreign Office, and the other is a Liverpool milkman. My father is a clergyman. He has always been the rector of a country village—well, ever since I've been around. He comes from the aristocratic side, if you like, and so it's been a funny mixture of the sort of low-income upbringing that you get where the father earns a very very low salary, but equally a very cultured upbringing in that it was part of an aristocratic heritage. And a very odd sort of attitude towards money because he came from a family that had a lot of money.

Mrs. Hurst: My father had no education at all, but he became a very successful journalist. He became the editor of a national newspaper. He was a fairly recent immigrant to this country from Northern Ireland. His father was a Northern Irish impoverished landowner, absolutely poorer than church mice. And my mother's American. She was brought up in New York, but she came here to get married and became a journalist. We never had any money either. But there was no conflict with the background because neither side of my family had the sort of inherited cultural assumptions about money that one side of Antony's did.

Mr. Hurst: We were both put through a very similar sort of education to each other for very different reasons. I was put through the public school and Oxbridge education because it was the natural thing for me. Whereas she was rather forced into it because that would represent an achievement for her parents.

Mrs. Hurst: "My daughter is going to have the best." And that is very much what happened. Oxford in my case. The

---

ABOUT THE PHOTOGRAPH:

Mrs. Hurst: It's nice because it's an attractive photograph. I think I can see things in that photograph which would strike people. For instance, Charlotte looks a bit withdrawn and suspicious. Miranda has a different way of looking shy.

Mr. Hurst: Miranda covers up shyness by looking aggressive and making a noise, whereas Charlotte covers up shyness by withdrawing and being quiet. That photograph almost overdoes that.

Mrs. Hurst: I think in a sense the photograph almost overdoes all of what I would call our "ruling characteristics."

Mr. Hurst: And that garden is a great deal smaller and less impressive than it looks in the photograph.

idea of a Crookshank going to Oxford was like man landing on the moon. But it had to be achieved to show the family had got somewhere.

Mr. Hurst: We have both suffered, I think, from being educated with a view to acquiring culture and knowledge. And certainly I feel that I missed out a lot on the sort of social contact field, partly because going to an all-male boarding school gives you a very limited cross-section to rub off on and partly because the ethos of the school made academic achievement the Number One god. So I think the risk is that we will lean over too far the other way and concentrate on giving our daughters the opportunity to have as much social contact as possible, and I think we'll probably assume that all the culture and the knowledge that they will want, they will pick up without much effort.

Mrs. Hurst: We've proposed to send our children to state schools, all other things being equal.

Mr. Hurst: Yes, but what we would want to check up on in the state school would be whether it had the atmosphere about it that was conducive to forming personal relationships and giving the girls an opportunity to pursue their own interests.

Mrs. Hurst: But I think probably we're both very concerned about finding out what makes us happy as people at the moment, and not too terribly bothered about laying down guidelines for the children. We would rather wait and see what turns up for them. It's not that we don't think about it.

Mr. Hurst: And very much let them do it their way rather than force them to do it the way we wished we had done it ourselves.

THREE WISHES:
Mrs. Hurst: I would like to have St. James Park at the end of the garden. I would like our street closed to all motorized traffic, and I would like this house to be three rooms deep instead of two rooms deep.

Mr. Hurst: I think I'll opt out of that question.

ANN AND BILL MARTIN
CHILDREN: TRACY, CAROL

MRS. MARTIN: Export manager
MR. MARTIN: Bus driver

Mrs. Martin: We're both from Perth, Scotland, but we met each other really in London. I've been here for nine years, and now when I go home I tend to find I can't stand all the talk and busybodying and all the gossip of a small community. It becomes petty to me and I'm not really interested in it any more. Now "coming home" is when I get into the lights of Euston Station.

I'm an export manager in a computer storage equipment firm. I love it. Very high-pressurized, you know. I am more or less my own boss because I run the whole complete exportation of our goods to every country in the world. I couldn't bear to be home all day. The kind of employment I have and the responsibility I have now as a young woman, I'd be lucky if I got that at fifty in Scotland. I mean I came down here on my own with Carol when she was a baby and didn't know what on earth I was coming down to. And I've made it as far as I'm concerned. I mean I'm a person in my own right. I'm an individual, I'm independent, I have a good salary. I think you'll find more of the Scots people who come down here—an awful lot of them are at the top in their careers and companies. I think Scots people are better workers, harder workers, more persistent, more reliable. Because we were brought up in an environment where there was no work. So if you have a job you have to hang on to it.

I came from a very poor family. For years up North there was unemployment, and my father had no skills. My mother was a charlady. Yes, definitely working-class. I was just lucky that my father made me study and stay on at school an extra year and take up commercial subjects, which I hated at the time, but which I'm glad for now. We were very poor, but very upright. Very religious. Catholic. I want some of the better things in life but I don't want them for nothing. I'm quite prepared to go out and get them, and I intend to have them. Not so much for myself, but I think everybody who has children likes to give them a better standard of living than they had themselves. Well, I think they should, too.

We intend to buy a house or a flat. I'd like it in the suburban London, not too far out, because I like London. I love London and it's been good to me financially and careerwise.

I think the only difference between the poor and the rich is us, the middle class. We're trying to keep our heads above water all the time because we are too proud. We don't want to accept things for nothing, and we have this feeling that we want to better ourselves. It's becoming harder and harder to keep to a decent standard of living or to better yourself. Sometimes I think you're better off being poorer-class because you get social security and you get all the free things—more things on the National Health, free milk for the children, free school dinners, you know.

ABOUT THE CHILDREN:
As they're daughters, I wouldn't like them to go out and think they're only going to be housewives and have babies. They may well do, but I'd like to think that if they do get married and have children, they'll always have another interest, a career.

Mr. Martin: When I left Scotland, employment was very low, jobs were hard to come by, and England was obviously where the money was. So I come to work here. I had two driving jobs before I become a bus driver. . . . Saw an advert on a bus. Wages sounded good. I've been there four years. If somebody would offer me a job at the same money doing something else—you know, a bit more interesting— I'd definitely take it. It gets a bit of a bore, really, just driving, driving, driving all day. I suppose the one thing I do miss is the social life I got used to in Scotland. Because back home, you know, I have so many friends. Sometimes when I go home they say to me, "Oh, I'm going golfing this Sunday," or "Going fishing next week," and things like this. This is the kind of thing I miss, you see. I find that the English pub is all sitting about just gossiping, whereas the Scots people like to get out and enjoy themselves a bit more—dancing, singing, music, you know. That's my idea of a good time.

THREE WISHES:

Mr. Martin: I'd like to run a business and live in the place of my choice. Of course if I win the pools or something like that we'll have a sixteen-room house in Perth. I was an apprentice glazier for about two or three years. I'd like to own a glazier shop. It seems like quite a small ambition, really, but it's something I've always fancied.

Question: How do you feel about your wife working?

Mr. Martin: I feel in London, if you really want to put something by for the future, I think you both have to work. But I know when Ann has a couple weeks off it's lovely coming home. Everything's done and tea's on. It's marvelous. But I do realize it's hard for her as well.

Mrs. Martin: It is a typical Scotsman who likes the wife as a housewife and to serve him, yes sir, no sir, three bags full.

ABOUT THE PHOTOGRAPH:

Mr. Martin: The picture looks a bit quiet. Yeah, it's rather posey. I think we're more of an active family than that suggests.

Mrs. Martin: It shows us as an informal, natural family, which I think we are.

Mrs. Martin: I think my husband prefers to dress more conservatively.

Mr. Martin: I usually wear a suit when I go out anywhere. To the local pub through the week, I only wear jeans. But otherwise, weekends, I always wear a suit.

ANNETTE AND GREGORY DESIR
CHILDREN: ALVINA, SABINA, DAMIAN, JANICE, PETER

MR. DESIR: Cook

Mrs. Desir: Well, I came to London from St. Lucia when I was seventeen. It's a small island in the West Indies. And I've been living in London for nearly twelve years now. I think we're more or less settled in London now, except probably there are times I feel like seeing my mom. She's still alive.

Mr. Desir: My father was over here and he asked me if I liked to come over. I left St. Lucia three years before my wife. Then I asked her to come over so we can get married, and she agreed. That was 1963. In the West Indies you hear about England and you think it is a paradise. That was my reason for coming over—to work, to earn a lot of money. And compared to the wages we used to get back home, I was quite satisfied.

It so happened my father was working here in the kitchen. And he gave me a job. And then I learned to be a chef through working in the kitchen. I like being a chef. It's quite interesting. I enjoy making Italian food. I like eating Italian food as well. Perhaps that's why I like making it. English food is simple to make. But you don't feel like you're achieving anything by making it.

Oh, we were thinking of one day going back home, but now it's out of the question because of the kids. If you go back you need a house or some place to put them and we don't have the money now. So we have to stay here for the time.

Mrs. Desir: Five years ago we became Jehovah's Witnesses. I remember we kept going from one church to another just looking, because we said to ourselves there is more to life than just living day after day without a hope, without anything to hold on to, and just having children. We got married twice, you know. Once in the Church of England and then we decided to go to the Catholic church. The Catholic church told us to get married again. The last church we went to was a Baptist church. But we felt there was something more so we kept searching, and we finally found Jehovah's Witnesses.

Mr. Desir: We have brought the children up with the Bible principles so we are hoping that they will live by it. Because all around us we can see the result of people who have rejected these principles—increase in violence and racial discrimination and these disturbances. So that's what we're looking forward to, that they will live according to the principles and when they grow up they will apply it to their life also and pass it on to their family, if they have any.

Mrs. Desir: It's built up our family. We are closer than we ever were before and we're happy. In fact, when we found the truth we were determined to have two children more. Before life was empty, you know, and we wished we never had any children.

THREE WISHES:

Mr. Desir: Well, we have wishes that no doubt will be fulfilled in the very near future, so I cannot say it is magical wishes. We're going to have peace and security and the end of war and wickedness. That is what God has promised with his son, Jesus Christ.

Mrs. Desir: We know we love everybody in our hearts. I am saying no matter how people feel against me I am going to put myself out and do my best to help them.

ABOUT THE PHOTOGRAPH:

Mrs. Desir: It's lovely. My husband usually has a tie on, but normally around the house that's what we're like.

Mr. Desir: She's always complimenting the kids on being very neat.

Mrs. Desir: Cleanliness is part of discipline, I think. Wouldn't you say? So I make an effort, and I do a lot of washing and always keep the children as neat as possible.

FIONA AND DAVID STURDY
CHILDREN: WILLIAM, TORROLD

MR. AND MRS. STURDY: Archaeologists

Mrs. Sturdy: My family was sort of a vaguely academic family. My father was really a geologist. He expected of me without question that I would go to university, preferably Oxford or Cambridge. Sort of substitute for a son. And you know I went to Birmingham, and read archaeology. Then I came back to London with a job at the British Museum.

I am not working now in archaeology, although every now and again I do do something. If I work and have to employ a nanny for the children, with the English system of taxation I cannot claim that back from what I earn. So, in fact, I end up out of pocket. When the children are grown up I'd like to do something. I think probably something quite different, perhaps dealing more with people rather than inanimate objects.

Mr. Sturdy: I was in Oxford all my life, the most provincial place there ever was. My father was a civil servant. I went to school there and university there and I worked there in a museum. In a sense I suppose I looked on London as a suburb of Oxford. I swore I'd never live in London and here I am.

I have a dream to live on a farm. It is obviously a dream that I'd be rather hard put to carry out. I did a period of actually carrying out this dream on my own for a time. My first house was a derelict farmhouse in a village just outside Oxford. The cows grazing on the green used to break through the front fence, and I was terrified they'd eat my yew tree.

ABOUT THE CHILDREN:
Mrs. Sturdy: I would like my children to be successful in whatever they do, not necessarily academic. I've perhaps seen too much of it. I'd quite like them to do something different, like Torrold saying today he wanted to be a zookeeper when he grew up, which actually would be a very super thing. You know, open-air life, being with animals, something practical and useful. There are an awful lot of academics I reckon that are really sort of drones.

Mr. Sturdy: When Torrold was born in University College Hospital, on the top floor of their maternity wards, I held him up looking down over London University and the British Museum, and I said, "One day, my boy, all this will be yours."

Question: How do you fit into the class system?

Mr. Sturdy: In social levels, in different parts of the country, you fit in different ways. In northern England you get asked out by a hospitable landowning class, which you never would under areas of greater population pressures. Around London a much wealthier landowning class maintains a much greater degree of privacy. . . . In London one feels more without a class. And traditionally in the country the church has provided some degree of social framework. In London, when I do go to church, it's conspicuous that my son and I form one sixth of the congregation. You know, twelve in a church built for two hundred people. So it's obviously a persistent breakdown when you move to London. But you crave the structure all the same.

Mrs. Sturdy: If we lived in the depth of the country, say we went to live in Westmoreland, we would have our place in society and we'd stick to it and we wouldn't have a great choice of friends. Whereas in London you can know more or less anyone, just as you meet people.

ABOUT THE PHOTOGRAPH:
Mrs. Sturdy: I think we look slightly goofy in both of them. . . . It's obvious we're archaeologists or something, isn't it? From the broken pot and that. . . . We collect things, but a bit of a mixture. Nothing particularly good.

Mr. Sturdy: Nothing particularly good, my foot. There's nothing desperately grand, but it's all quite interesting.

Mrs. Sturdy: None of those things are museum pieces.

Mr. Sturdy: The Greek altar is, vaguely.

ANN AND ERNIE LEE
CHILDREN: JOANNE, JANET, ANTONY

MRS. LEE: Community worker
MR. LEE: Gardener for the local duke

Mrs. Lee: I have lived in Pimlico all my life. My mother was born here as well, in the street that I live in now, and my father was born in Fulham, not far from here. My grandmother was born here too. There's only one cousin that's ever gone beyond the immediate area.

My ·grandmother looked after me until I was about fifteen because my mother always had to work. I loved being a child here. It was sort of a village atmosphere really, right in London. It's not as strong now, obviously, because a lot of the buildings have been pulled down. And some people have moved away. But a good percentage of the children that I knew are still around with their own families.

My life has been centered around this area. If I can't get somewhere by walking, I really don't want to go. All my friends are here. I hate traveling, so that I never go on holiday unless I'm forced to.

I'd fight very hard to stay here if anybody wants to move me. I don't like the country anyway, and the suburban areas around London leave me cold. And the thing I like about it best is the fact that I can look out my window and see my kids playing with the kids of· people I played with as a child. Also, you get such a variety of people. You can go from a very low kind of living to the very highest.

I would say we're right smack in the middle. We're not poor, because we both work very hard, and we both, I think, believe in a hard day's work for your pay. I don't think either of us would ever appreciate or want to be rich. Neither of us, for instance, ever craved to own our own house. We like to think that we can enjoy our money with things that make us happy. Ernie likes his stereo and his motorbike. I just like to be able to buy things I like.

Really, I'm a qualified librarian, which I was for seven years until Antony was born. And then I did a variety of jobs, but mainly looked after other people's children and cleaning, domestic work, because I could take my kids with me. But for the last fifteen months I've worked at the Neighborhood Aid Center as a volunteer coordinator. I happen to like people, so if I can help, I want to.

I'll go back to being a librarian when the children are older. I always wanted to be a librarian, always.

Mr. Lee: When I was very young, sort of about ninish, I used to be very mad on collecting cactus, hundreds and hundreds of all different sorts. And I was always very interested in flowers. Then, when I was older, I took a job in a park over at Battersea to see if I liked it, for six months. It seemed to suit me. And I went to night school, a day college, passed the usual sort of exams and things. Plus the fact that I did lots of private jobs for people around this area, moneyed people who wanted a particular garden laid out for them. That's how I became a gardener.

Now I work for a duke. Gardener, tree-trimmer, is what's sort of on the book. Our job is mainly to lay out new gardens and keep them intact. I guess a laborer could do the job, but there again he wouldn't know one plant from another. I like the job. For a start, I like working out in the open air. And we don't do the same job twice. So you never get bored. And when you're tree-pruning, you can get up there and get rid of all your aggravation on the saw.

ABOUT THE PHOTOGRAPH:

Mrs. Lee: To look at the photograph quickly, you'd think it was three different kids from three separate families. But when you look carefully, they're really alike.

Mr. Lee: I look like Jesus Christ. People looking at it will say, "My God." And I'll say, "Yeah, that's me."

Mrs. Lee: I'll tell you what I do notice. You couldn't tell that Ernie's a gardener. No, I would have said he's an actor.

Mr. Lee: Or a hermit.

BRIDIE AND JOHN RYAN
CHILD: ANNETTE

MR. RYAN: Plasterer

As a boy I lived in Ireland. Tipperary. I was fifteen when I left so I'm here over eight, nine years now. Most of my brothers and sisters were over here, you know, so I came over to them. In Ireland you hear of all the big money in London and all this. I went home about three years ago and I stayed there a fortnight, and you know, I just didn't fit in any more.

But I'd like my kid to be brought up in Ireland. For one, it's my personal opinion, I think the schools are much better in Ireland. And the way of life is much better for them. And houses—ninety-nine percent of the people have their own houses in Ireland. I'm talking about the country part in Ireland. I didn't know what a flat was until I come over here.

I think people are much friendlier in Ireland. That's the way I like it, you know. When I come over here, you learn very fast to keep to yourself. Well, there's millions of people in London, but sometimes you can be very lonely.

We're thinking of going back to Ireland in maybe two years, before Annette starts school, because I wouldn't like her to be going to a school where there's say ninety-nine percent of the kids are foreigners, colored kids, right? I think myself that the standard of education dropped in this country over the last eight years. Dropped a hell of a lot. Well, to me anyway, a colored kid is not as brainy as a white kid, you know. So they have to lower the standard of education to cope with them.

I think the point is instead of the colored people getting a raw deal, I think the white person is getting a raw deal. Like the housing situation. There might be, say, six thousand white people, English people, on the waiting list. Then these Asians come to this country and you have them dropping in the queue. And you begin to ask yourself, why should they get housing while other English people are living in slums? This I cannot understand.

But I think the colored person did one good turn for the Irish people in this country. Like the prejudice, it shifted over to them. Like they're foreigners, and we're now accepted as kind of a second-grade English person.

The only thing I'd ask of Annette was that she wouldn't marry a colored bloke. That's the way I feel about it.

I do plastering now. I must say it's a tough job. I like it very much, but it wouldn't be everybody's cup of tea, you know. You see, I used to be a bus conductor, and one day I said, "This is no good for me." Being a plasterer is a lot more interesting. I think this job is the best I've had so far. You take a lot more care in it, and you get satisfaction out of doing a good job. The blokes I work with are craftsmen, and it's good to watch blokes doing the job when they know what they're doing.

Mrs. Ryan: I've been to Ireland. Everyone in my family was born over there except me. I've got a sister living there. But I don't know whether I'd like to live there.

I was born in Victoria, not far from here. Years ago most people didn't have television, so in the evenings people who had children used to sit at the door and watch the children play. Oh, it's different now. Now you can go out and you mightn't meet anyone you know for days. Because they've pulled a lot of the houses down, and most of the people I know, they've got married and live miles outside London.

My mother was a nurse. My father had asthma, so he was only a messenger. He was civil service but he could only do a light job because he'd get sick. Before Annette was born, I was a clerical assistant in the civil service. But I like being a mother more.

We go to Mass every Sunday, and most Saturdays we go see friends of mine. We like to spend our holidays by the sea or in the country. Last year we went to a holiday camp. First time we've ever been. And we had a smashing time. Annette was allowed to go into the dance hall in the evenings with us till ten, and she won first prize in the baby contest. It was that Annette enjoyed herself so much that we did.

I want Annette to live a proper life and to not get into any serious trouble. And to meet somebody nice to marry.

IDA AND GEORGE GRAY

MRS. GRAY: Part-time worker in canteen
MR. GRAY: Retired painter, Ministry of Works

Mrs. Gray: I first came to Pimlico when I was six weeks old, from Streatham. My father was born in Pimlico. There were seven children. My father was a chef, first of all on the trains and then for a company. My father used to let our anterooms for four shillings. And he often had to put money in to help pay the taxes and rates. You kept tenants for years. You wouldn't have that these days, would you?

I had a very lucky childhood and teenage. My mother never had to go to work. We had a holiday every year, and when my father was on the trains, I think we all used to go to Southend for half a crown.

During the war, we were often blasted out here. We had no gas, no lights, no nothing, no windows. Everybody used to come down here in the house away from the top. Some nights they slept in the coal cellar—the council put bunks in the coal cellar. I never slept out there with my father because we had the basement flat.

We've tried to get out of Pimlico a number of times, but we just don't have the money. We would love to live at the sea. We thought when George retired we'd have enough money, but it's just sad that we didn't. I'll tell you what would have been nice. Ten years ago, had we known George was going to get a pension, had we known he was going to get a lump sum and that sort of thing, with our savings gone in it, we could have got something when we retired.

But we're contented here, though we could do with another room. We still haven't got a bathroom. We've never had a bathroom, either one of us. We have to go to the public baths. But you get used to these things so that you don't take any notice of it.

Oh, I think I know everybody in Pimlico. When we come back from a holiday, George always said, "Oh, that was lovely. You didn't know anybody." I have lived here for sixty-six years—of course I know people. George could walk around for hours and wouldn't speak to a soul.

I say this, I think as we've grown older, we are very very contented. We don't ask for a lot. We like our summer holiday—we've just had another week in Eastbourne. As I am walking often through the park, Battersea Park, I often say, "Aren't we lucky, George!"

THREE WISHES:
One, good health. I think your health is everything. Two, I have a niece who is mental and I pray that she will be right one day. My third wish is that we have a good many years together.

Mr. Gray: I was born in King's Cross, and I came to Pimlico when I was very young. My father was a packer and he was in the South African war, and he was in the reserve when I left school. I left school just before I was fourteen, before I should have done.

I was unemployed for part of the Depression. Yes, Chadwick Street Labour Exchange, there were queues out there. They used to let them in every quarter of an hour in those days. All day that used to go on.

I was called up in 1941 when I was twenty-nine or thirty. Before that I was a painter. After the Second World War, I first met my wife. When we got married, we weren't very young. So we never had children.

THREE WISHES:
I, too, would wish for good health. Two, a little cottage or a house at the seaside, and three, to go on just as we are going on now.

ABOUT THE PHOTOGRAPH:

Mr. Gray: I wish I'd taken my glasses off so you wouldn't have all the reflection in the glasses. Otherwise, I think it's all right. It would have been better with my coat on.

Mrs. Gray: I think the photographs are life-like. I think this one is like me. It even shows my deformity. I have to wear a steel support for my tummy, you know. He spoilt the photo because he hadn't a coat on.

WINIFRED AND ALFRED JOHNSTONE

MR. JOHNSTONE: Museum porter
MRS. JOHNSTONE: Domestic helper

(Mr. Johnstone not interviewed)

Mrs. Johnstone: I suppose I would consider myself a Londoner after all of these years, wouldn't I? Many years ago I came to London from Eastbourne. I can't remember how old I was. I was married at twenty-three, and now that's thirty-nine years in July, the fifteenth. So it's a long way back, isn't it?

My oldest son lives at Stepney. He's a regular soldier, you see. He came out of the army but he is still a soldier, so that if there were a war he'd be called straight back. Thank God there isn't a war. We don't want any of that business, do we? Had enough. My other son is married, in Bristol. He's a plumber and he's working for himself now. And I lost my daughter, you see. I'm afraid I'm rather selfish about it, but I miss my children terribly. I wish I'd hear from them a bit more, but I suppose they've got their lives to lead. I think every parent feels the same.

I sometimes wish I had a garden, but apart from that I'm really very happy in London. It's quite a happy place here. Everybody is very friendly and nice, which is a great advantage, isn't it? In this building, which is council, most people I come up against are very nice people, very pleasant. I think it depends on the way you treat people. If you're nice to people they're nice to you. That's how I have always found life.

I have worked on and off all my life. I work for a children's novelist who lives around the corner here. I do all kinds of things like cleaning, helping with bringing the wines. I've been with her for twenty-six years.

My husband and I both work hard. He's sort of porter at Burlington House. He opens the door. Today he's going to open the door to the Queen of Denmark, and I am going to this reception. After I leave you, I am going off to Piccadilly to see her.

If I could wish for anything, I would like a little house in the country with a garden. That's what I would like. But it's not to be, I don't think. Well, it's so difficult to get a place, isn't it? And my husband's got to think of his bread and butter. After all, he's sixty-one, and he's got to wait a while before he retires. Still, anything could happen before then, couldn't it?

MARGARET AND RICHARD HODGE
CHILD: SARA

MRS. HODGE: Nanny now working in a nursery school
MR. HODGE: Policeman

Mr. Hodge: I grew up in North London. One sister, quite a normal upbringing, I suppose. That's the best I could describe it. Fortunately, I wasn't aware of the Second World War, so therefore that was no problem. I can appreciate for those that it did affect. Probably it left a bad memory.

When I think back I don't know why I became a policeman. Probably saw something advertised or whatever. I think the only thing I could say that made me choose this type of activity is I dislike working indoors. Being inside ten minutes is about long enough, quite honestly.

Well, if one was to go by all the advertising, you'd believe it was a far more glamorous, dangerous, exciting job than it actually is. I mean, ninety-nine percent of the job is as routine as any other job.

I cover the whole of this area, Pimlico. Being a professional police officer is more or less being a professional community relations officer. You know, you don't make enemies when you deal with people. You attempt to make friends with them.

Mrs. Hodge: Well, I was an orphan, and I was brought up with the Church of England Children's Society. I had always from a small child wanted to be a children's nurse. And so I went straight on to my training with the Church of England Children's Society. And then I had had so much institution that I thought I wanted to break out and be a nanny. But really, this didn't work out very well for me, because when you live in as a nanny you sort of become part of the family but you're neither family or employee. You see these nannies in Hyde Park, fifty or sixty years old, and you know they've been doing it all their lives and it's very sad that these nannies never had their own children. So I got my own flat in London and did daily nannying, which I found much more satisfactory because you could lead your own life.

Well, I always worked up till I had Sara, and then Richard doesn't really like the idea of me working. But the thing is, I feel when you're a housewife you become a bit of a cabbage and I think it does get me out and it gives me just that little break.

Now I teach at a nursery school which is in Pimlico. The school is held in a church hall and I teach there a couple of mornings a week. I enjoy it, and also I can take Sara.

It's too far to think like this, but as Richard says, basically I want Sara to know how to cope with life. And I want her to feel she's secure. This is an obsession with me really, because I suppose I lacked it as a child. But to feel that whatever the problems, she's got a home, she's got parents. And I feel education is important.

THREE WISHES:
One is that I would like a car, to be able to afford and run a car. I think it would help us to enjoy life a bit more by being able to get out. Two, I would like the country to be without strikes and wage problems. Three, I would like a son to go with my daughter.

ABOUT THE PHOTOGRAPH:

Mr. Hodge: As I've learned from experience in my particular job, if you accept people as you see them, then you always get the wrong impression of them. And just to see a photograph of somebody and automatically form an opinion of that person would be completely false anyway. All you're reproducing there is a person's look for a second. What appears behind the façade may be completely different.

Mrs. Hodge: Being the house-proud person that I am, I like the photograph, because it does show off a little bit of the furniture. But somehow or other I would get the completely wrong impression of us from that photograph. I think we're too far apart. We look as though we've just had a great argument or something. We have our ups and downs, but the three of us are really very close.

JOSEPHINE AND DAVID JEFFCOCK
CHILDREN: JOHN, GEORGE, CORDELIA, VENETIA

MR. JEFFCOCK: Stockbroker

Mrs. Jeffcock: The sitting-down photograph I like best of all but it's one hundred years out of date. And I think we are one hundred years out of date, but I don't mind.

Mr. Jeffcock: It's the pose that hasn't changed.

Question: Is your life one hundred years old or contemporary?

Mrs. Jeffcock: It has got all the discomforts of contemporary life . . .

Mr. Jeffcock: With none of its advantages.

Mrs. Jeffccok: Yes, a few of its advantages.

Mr. Jeffcock: But I have never wished to live in the past. I wouldn't like to live any other time but now. Our ancestors were much more frightened of what was going to happen than we are.

Mrs. Jeffcock: The luxury has gone that we would have had one hundred years ago. One the other hand, one isn't tied like one would have been one hundred years ago. That one had dinner at eight. Now one can have dinner at six or one can have dinner at ten or one needn't have dinner at all.

Mr. Jeffcock: Yes, life is very much less formal than it was. People don't mind what you do. To a certain extent I don't think they ever have. But one hundred years ago the form was more important than it is now.

Mrs. Jeffcock: Having visiting cards and that sort of thing. That life is completely gone.

ABOUT THE PHOTOGRAPH:

Question: Would strangers get the right idea?

Mr. Jeffcock: People would get the completely wrong idea but it's the one that we try desperately hard to give (*laughter*). But I mean, in a way they would get quite the right idea.

Mrs. Jeffcock: But they would get the right wrong idea . . .

Mr. Jeffcock: They would get the right idea but it wouldn't be what they imagined, if you understand what I mean. Well, if you show a photograph of a man and a woman relatively well dressed, with four tidy children and in a comfortable drawing room on a large sofa with a dog sprawling on the floor and some pretty furniture, you get an impression of great elegance which is much more apparent to somebody who doesn't live in it than to those who do.

Mrs. Jeffcock: You don't see the cigarette burns on the sofa . . .

Mr. Jeffcock: No. And you don't know that the floor creaks and there's a bookcase around the corner which doesn't fit. But ostensibly, that is a very elegant-looking room.

CHICAGO

JANICE AND RICHARD WETZEL

MRS. WETZEL: Art teacher and painter
MR. WETZEL: Art teacher and painter

Mr. Wetzel: As a painter Chicago is a good place for me, for all the reasons that it's a bad place for someone in that profession. Well, art done in Chicago is usually relatively small-scale and very personal in scale, in terms of its content, as opposed to sort of international style, which is currently marketable and acceptable. That's the kind of thing in art that interests me—that kind of personal investigation scale, rather than formal investigations. And so this is an ideal place. It feeds my attitude. And yet in terms of career and recognition, it's a very bad place to be in that it is not stylish or acceptable anywhere but here. The market here is very small.

I can afford to have these views because I also teach art. Teaching gives me the freedom to pursue my own tack, maybe not the kind of depth I would like or with the kind of time and full commitment that I would like, but at least I don't have to compromise any of the really important things, just a little psychological comfort. If I were seriously looking to make a comfortable living as an artist, I would have to really do a lot more of paying attention to trends and trying to second-guess what comes next.

I still believe in the truth of the idea that if you do something that's worthy of note and which is authentically important, it will eventually be seen for that. And so the way I structure things here, with the teaching taking care of the financial obligations and the mundane things, I'm doing the very best I can with my work. And if it happens that the best I can do turns out to be good enough, then it's important stuff. If not, it has been important for me, and I haven't had to give it up.

Mrs. Wetzel: All of my four grandparents came from Sweden. I grew up in a Swedish community in the South Side of Chicago. My mother moved into a house there when she was two years old, and we lived in that house until I moved to this neighborhood so there were some really deep roots there.

Extended family? I guess we were in a way. But extended family sounds real warm and friendly; I think of something very Italian, very black, perhaps Jewish where there's a real closeness, a familial kind of thing. And our family, being northern, to this day isn't like that. I never saw people kiss each other as much until I really got out of that community. Swedish Lutheran Church and the whole business.

I love my job. I teach art in an inner-city high school, in the ghetto, and it's very stimulating. My own painting is relatively nonexistent these days. I think the trouble is, I spend all my energy at school and I just have very little of whatever creative force there is by the time I come home.

I have no interest in a family or children, but I can feel a lot for my kids at school. I mean they're *my* kids. I feel like perhaps I am contributing something. Really, I think I teach them more about human relations than anything else. I don't like teaching in a middle-class white environment. That's what I grew up in and it's very boring to me.

Mrs. Wetzel: I'm very content with my lot in life.

Mr. Wetzel: Yeah. We don't have the American Dream about getting rich and then getting richer. We've been married ten years.

Mrs. Wetzel: And it's been sort of uphill ever since.

Mr. Wetzel: Everything has fallen into place very nicely.

ABOUT THE PHOTOGRAPH:

Mrs. Wetzel: That painting in the photograph is a link with the past. I blew up an old photograph of my mother as an infant and painted it from that.

Mr. Wetzel: You know that particular painting was in a student exhibit in the hallway of the Art Institute. I saw it and it sort of knocked me out. It fascinated me, and I found out who did it. A whole kind of professional-respect thing happened around the painting that made me want to meet Janice on that level. I think it had something to do with us getting together. That was probably twelve or thirteen years ago.

EVA AND NESTOR HERNANDEZ
CHILDREN: LETITIA (TISHA), NESTOR
DOG: JOI

MR. HERNANDEZ: Counselor for former mental patients

Mrs. Hernandez: I was born in Puerto Rico, but I came to New York when I was a little baby. We grew up in Manhattan. My mother was very strict. At eight o'clock I was upstairs in the house. When I was fourteen years old, we came to Chicago. When we came here, me and my sister cried because our feet were frozen and everything. In New York the snow doesn't turn to ice like it does here. Well, I like it here now. I don't like the weather but everything else I like.

We just got back from a trip to Puerto Rico. I really enjoyed it. But I felt a little foreign. Everyone was talking Spanish so well. And, you know, I know how to speak Spanish but I don't speak it as well as they do in Puerto Rico. Over here everybody talks the same kind of Spanish. And we understand each other. But over there you can't really express yourself the way you really want to.

ABOUT THE CHILDREN:
I'd like them to go to college and that. To become something. To do things we could never do, you know. Like Tisha—I don't want her to just get married. I'd like her to take some kind of trade or learn something. And not just to be a housewife. If I were to do things over I would have thought more about school. Right now I don't know how to do anything, really. If I were doing something, I'm sure the kids wouldn't get in my hair so much. I would like to learn how to do things, like typing well. And I would like to travel. That's fun.

Mr. Hernandez: I've been around this general area for a good twenty years. I come from a family of five children. I'm the oldest. They're very religious. They belong to the Pentecostal church. And I'm what you might say the black sheep of the family. Because I don't go to church. Like my mother says, I'm the son of the Devil, because I don't go to church and stuff like that. But what the heck. In other ways I'm the black sheep too. 'Cause my brother is going to college, you know, and he plans on finishing the whole shot. Which I never did. I went one year and that was it.

I was born in Puerto Rico, and we left when I was five years old. You know, I feel very Puerto Rican. If you don't feel what you are, then you're being a fake to yourself. I mean I'm a United States citizen, yes. And I'm an American, yes. But I'm a Puerto Rican also. Yes. I feel very Puerto Rican.

Like any parent, I don't want my kids to get into a lot of trouble, jail and stuff like that. Basically all kids are good, you know. It's just that some have a lot of problems and they don't know how to deal with them and then they start getting into trouble.

I enjoy my job. I work with a rehabilitation center for the emotionally disturbed. You're dealing with ex-mental patients. I have certain cases and I counsel them. And I run a thrift shop which is part of the agency. And I try to train them to basically be able to go out and get a job on their own and learn certain basic work skills and get them ready for job placement.

I don't know what I'll be doing ten years from now. When you plan on things and you start wishing and dreaming, then things don't turn out the way you want them to and it's a big downfall, you know. I think the best way to do it is just live life. Like when you get to that bridge you'll cross it. Like the vacation to Puerto Rico. I've been wanting to go for a good ten, fifteen years. And every time that I've decided that I was going to go, always another problem came up. Well, this time I really didn't have the money, but I said to myself, if I keep waiting for this I'll never go. So I went and borrowed some money and we just packed up our things and went. Now I'm paying back the loan, but at least we did what we wanted to.

There's been good times and there's been bad times. There's a lot of better times ahead. I'm pretty sure.

BARBARA WARREN
CHILDREN: REBECCA, MATTHEW

MS. WARREN: Executive secretary

When I moved into this area nine years ago, I kind of did it because of the children being black. Matthew was about six months old when we moved in. I felt more comfortable here. The people didn't question you if you were a single woman with children. My very very close friends I've met in this area.

I grew up on the Far North Side of Chicago. I guess it was considered suburban when I was living out there. It was a very happy childhood. I felt very safe living in the city. The one thing that's been the hardest for me to come to grips with is that the city is no longer safe. There's so much more happening on the streets now than there was when I was a child.

This last Christmas, twice in the same week I got mugged. The first time they took my purse and raped me. The second time it was another bunch of kids. They beat me up and just grabbed my purse. From that point on I became deathly afraid. But that basically is the hardest thing for me to realize: the fact that we're living in a city that is now dangerous.

My father was a policeman here in Chicago. My mother is from England. I guess I'm completely opposite from what they intended me to turn out to be. I used to be very strait-laced and very very shy. And then when I got out of high school I was bound and determined to change. And I moved out of the house. And then having the children and my children being black was like, "What have we ever done to deserve this?" But I did things the way I wanted to do them and I'm very happy I did.

My father passed away a year and a half ago. Now, the interesting thing is, my parents have accepted my children and have been closer to my children more than they have to any of their grandchildren. My father was terribly fond of Matthew and Rebecca. There was just nothing that he couldn't do for them. He just loved them dearly. But then, I think I relied on my parents more because I was alone. I don't know. I think the whole process was a learning process for me and my parents at the same time.

ABOUT THE CHILDREN:
I've told Matthew that whatever he chooses to do, just do it well. I hope that things'll be better for them. I hope that they'll be able to walk down the street at ten o'clock at night and not be afraid. And I hope my son never has to go and fight a war. Basically, I just hope they're happy.

THREE WISHES:
I thought I wanted financial security, money. I'm not quite sure about that. I think I'd like to have a little bit more than I have now, for the children's sake. Secondly, I wish there was more happiness in the world. You don't see many people laugh and carry on. And I wish I was married right now. I think that's what I basically want more than anything. It's just something I think I'm ready for, something I feel that I've missed. I went to my first encounter group last night and I was told that the idea of marriage is becoming an obsolete thing in our society—that it is something that you shouldn't really need.

ABOUT THE PHOTOGRAPH:
I think strangers would get a pretty good idea of us. I see a lot of things in the picture that other people could see. I think it shows a lot of closeness between the three of us. I mean I get a definite feeling of happiness and a lot of warmth. Especially with Rebecca, I get a sense of real security. And I think Matthew looks the same way too. He's kind of standing very straight, like he's assuming the role of the man in the family. There's just the three of us, so in a lot of ways Matthew does assume the responsibility of a man in the house. Or at least now he's trying to because he's getting old enough to. Especially where Rebecca is concerned. He likes to watch out for her in a lot of ways. . . . Basically that's a very honest picture. I didn't prepare for it in any way. My house looks like this all the time. I'm a chronic cleaner-upper.

When you say you want to get married everyone automatically thinks, "Ah, she wants the house in the suburbs, and the second car and the color TV sets." I don't want that. If I got married I'd probably stay exactly where I am and still continue to work.

About this encounter group. A lot of women are just getting together and they seem to have this feeling that if you're a woman, you're automatically born with these problems that you have to overcome. And I feel like wow, you know, I've overcome quite a few of them already. I really have.

One of the girls last night at our meeting said, "Before we get started, I just want to tell you that this friend of mine is having a seminar on "'How to drop out of the nine-to-five job and survive by other means.'" And I said, "Oh, I just got back into a nine-to-five job and I'm so happy you wouldn't believe it!" You see, I worked up until Rebecca was six months old. And that's when I dropped out. And I went on welfare for three years. And that was a horrendous experience. I had never even known about welfare and I really had a lot of guilt feelings about going on it. In one way, it was a happy experience because I was with the children. I saw my daughter grow up. But I really cannot recommend it for anyone. You really don't have much to live on. And if your check is one day late . . . I cleaned house for friends of mine to supplement my income.

Then when Rebecca was old enough to send to Head Start, I said, "The hell with it." And I just got up and I went back to work. I went back with the thought in mind that "I'm going to be self-sufficient. I'm not going to rely on anybody for anything."

Now I'm an executive secretary, which is just like a fairly recent promotion. And I feel very happy with my job. I'm extremely happy.

Question: Can you put yourself in a class?

It's hard for me to fit myself into a class. First of all because my family had money. When I went on welfare it was a complete and utter shock to them. I think if I hadn't quit working, I would have just become a very middle-class type of person with very middle-class-type ideas. But if you go on welfare you begin to meet people with real problems. You really get an insight into, you know, it's tough out there. It's very very tough. But I still have middle-class ideas about a lot of things. Like if I have company I still set the table the way my mother sets the table.

Like Matthew asked me the other day, "Are we poor rich people or are we rich poor people?" Because he knows his grandmother has money, and he knows if he wants a new bike I can't give it to him right now. So it's hard to put myself in a class. It really is.

BRUNO AND BEATRICE BERTUCCI
CHILDREN: ANNA, PIA

MRS. BERTUCCI: Public aid representative
MR. BERTUCCI: School teacher

Mr. Bertucci: Almost four years ago, we saw an ad in the paper for this apartment building, and it was federally subsidized rent. We were living in a small apartment in a suburb . . .

Mrs. Bertucci: And found the suburb very boring.

Mr. Bertucci: North Riverside. I mean it was beautiful, typically beautiful, but we hated it. It was so boring.

Mrs. Bertucci: The focus of the whole suburban thing, you know, was you spent your time between where you lived and the shopping centers. My family, my parents, and my sister lived there, so we were close to my family there, and it felt very confining.

Mr. Bertucci: It was a funny thing, you know, with all the wide-open spaces and everything we felt more confined than we do here in the city.

Mrs. Bertucci: I don't think *neighborhood* in the old traditional sense exists in this part of Chicago. I mean where most of the people have common backgrounds, they've lived in the neighborhood for a long time, they know each other very well.

Mr. Bertucci: You see, when you say *neighborhood*, that means something much more emotional to each of us because we both, you know, came from the old ethnic neighborhoods. Mine was a mixture of Italian, Irish, and German. But it was definitely a place where businesses had gone back to grandparents. Where I grew up, on Twenty-sixth Street and Canal, there was a church that everybody participated in, in one way or another, because most of us went to this Catholic school. And the neighborhood was then very sharply defined by the boundaries of your parish. Whereas here we don't go to church any more, so we don't have that

definition any more. Now, we tend to define the boundaries of neighborhood by the friends that we've met and where they live.

My family was very large, interdependent, Italian. It kept you to a strict norm. And if you deviated from it you tended to be considered eccentric. I was. Yes, I was bookish. And I didn't identify at all as an Italian-American.

My father was a tavernkeeper. Traditionally, most of my relatives have worked for the city of Chicago. You ask if I grew up as intended. Well, if I had I would be driving a truck or working as a laborer for the city of Chicago.

Mrs. Bertucci: I grew up on the West Side, and it was similar in the sense that it was largely Bohemian, Polish, German. I think you always tend to look back on that kind of thing with nostalgia. I suppose if you were looking at it very hardheadedly and realistically, I know that I would not really enjoy it now or get along very well in that kind of surrounding.

Mr. Bertucci: When we were growing up, the focus of all our social outlooks was family, and we wanted to meet other people. Which we did when we moved here.

Mrs. Bertucci: My family was, let's say, upwardly mobile, middle-working-class family. And there were always expectations for the children to go to school, you know, to eventually go to college. But the expectations for the girls in my family were really to eventually marry and be a housewife, period. Which really was not my expectation. When I was about twelve years old, my parents moved to the suburbs. My father was a printer, linotype operator, and enjoyed it, I guess, although he worked awfully hard. Most of my memories of my father when I was a child were his dashing home from work, swallowing his supper, and running off to his second job in the evening. It was pretty rough on him, I imagine.

My mother speaks Bohemian fluently. It's a curious situation because she is about third-generation Czech. My father was born in Czechoslovakia but doesn't speak a word of it. He had a very heavy reaction when he was about fifteen years old, when he came over, and promptly forgot everything. So we used to have these situations where my mother would speak Bohemian with my grandmother, his mother, and he would speak to her in English.

ABOUT THE CHILDREN:

Mr. Bertucci: I would like to see them grow up to be capable, independent young women, who would marry late if they choose to marry. And I secretly hope that they would consider it well. I would like to see them find some occupation or avocation that's satisfying. It wouldn't be a question of income or prestige but whether they would feel fulfilled in it.

Mrs. Bertucci: That's pretty close to the way I feel.

When we were married, Bruno and I had the same educational background approximately, and I always felt a kind of inequality because Bruno was working and I wasn't, and I thought that I should be able to. And so it really means a great deal to me to be able to work now. I just started, in fact, about a year ago. I'm reviewing the work of the caseworkers in the district public aid offices. I am not really a social worker. I was glad to be able to get something to support the family almost entirely. It also means a great deal to me that Bruno was able to get out of the public schools and get into what he wants to get into.

Mr. Bertucci: I never took an official leave of absence from teaching, but I have only been substituting this past year, whenever we needed the money. I've worked since I was thirteen, you know, I've always paid my way, and this is the first time I've had such a long time without working. I am using my year off for thinking, reviewing what I want to do for a career. Teaching was frustrating in the sense that I always thought my talents were barely used. I would like to have a job that I could take home at night, that could keep me up at night thinking about solutions.

Question: Can you put yourself in a class?

Mr. Bertucci: As I said, it's fashionable for people our age and our background to reject the middle class. But I think we don't fit into the middle class. For one thing, the middle class acquires possessions. We like to have things that are useful and if they're not useful, we don't like them around.

Mrs. Bertucci: According to our income, we are middle-class, and I'm sure according to some values, we are typically middle-class, if middle-class orientation is to devote a lot of attention to your children.

Mr. Bertucci: To get their teeth fixed and have their throat cultures taken. Although I'm sure even lower classes would do that if they had the means to.

ABOUT THE PHOTOGRAPH:

Mr. Bertucci: I think we may have been more relaxed if we didn't prepare for being photographed, but we did. We wanted a formal photograph.

Mrs. Bertucci: The kids love dressing up, and we like dressing up once in a while. And we'd never had a formal portrait taken.

Mr. Bertucci: And also we'd spent considerable time before that looking at old family photographs.

Mrs. Bertucci: That's right. We spent several weekends looking at old family photographs.

Mr. Bertucci: We thought after sixty years, what survives in a photograph are the little details that people took time to put in there. Well, we wanted a formal man-in-a-suit type of photograph. I like to keep a certain formality, to keep distance between myself and other people that I can bridge when I want. For example, I would hate to work at a job where I was on a first-name basis. I would like to be as formal as the English could be.

LILY AND THOMAS WALTON
MR. WALTON: Retired bus driver

(Mrs. Walton not interviewed)

Well, the wife, she was born in England, in Hull, but she lived in Canada. When the war broke out in 1914 she was on a vacation in Hull. And then, of course, she couldn't get back to Canada. Where I worked and my father worked was a big paint and varnish company in Hull. My wife's brother worked in the same place too. So he went to the war and I went to the war, and then naturally they took all the women they could get to fill in these jobs. And she went to work in the paint company. And then after the war I came back to the paint and varnish company. I went back driving, they call them lorries there, we call them trucks. And I met her and then, like I say, we got married in Hull. I got out of the army in 1919 and we got married in the same year.

The wife came from Toronto, see? And she worked for, it's a branch of the Edison Company. She made these electric bulbs. And naturally she wanted to get back again. So we got married in a hurry and took off. And then we stayed in Toronto for five years with her sister and husband for a while and then we got our own apartment from there. We stayed in Canada five years and then we could get over into this country.

I was on the streetcars for a while in Toronto. And then the manager came from New York with four buses when we first started buses in Toronto. And he found out that I had drove lorries all the time in England and so he got me to volunteer to go on these buses and get them rolling. We had a tough superintendent there, and he said that the buses wouldn't last a month anyway and you'd be out of a job. Well, this manager from New York said, "Don't worry. They'll go over." And he said, "I'll make you a guarantee. If they don't, you can come to New York and I'll give you a better job than what you have." So I took it. Yeah, boy, they got hundreds of buses there now!

I was a bus driver in Chicago for twenty-one years. Nope, I didn't retire. We had no pension and we had very little benefits. So I quit. Then after I left I went to a bank in Chicago, and I was chauffeur for thirteen years with the vice chairman at that time. And then the reason I left the bank was they brought in a new rule, at sixty-five you had to retire. And I was sixty-nine at the time, so I had to go. Yeah, I've been driving all my life. That's all I've done. Once in a while I get my son's car if they go on vacation. Well, they have two, and I bring one here. I always liked the idea of driving.

So I've been retired now, let's see, nearly—this'll be the tenth year now. Well, it gets monotonous. And especially during the bad weather here. Summertime I play golf, so that kills a little monotony there. And I'm president of the council in this building here. That's one thing that keeps me busy. And like I say, we have these meetings and then we've had twenty-five die in this building in five years. That makes five a year, so we've got funerals to take care of. A lot of these people are by themselves. I'm lucky I have my wife here. But I'm the only couple on this entire floor. . . . In these CHA buildings you get reduced rent. It took us five and a half years to get into this place.

I like Chicago, but I still like me old England. I still have two sisters here, both in Hull. They say once you like a country like England, you always have that feeling. I think that's true.

THREE WISHES:
I don't know. Everything's going well. I'll be seventy-nine in November.

ABOUT THE PHOTOGRAPH:

Mr. Walton: Oh yes. I think it's a very good picture of both of us. Yeah, I think strangers would get the right idea about us. Don't you? That's the way I usually dress. The bobby? Well, that's a London bobby. I bought that in London on me way back last time I was there. Which is three years ago now.

EVELYN AND ORIN WALKER
CHILDREN: MELVIN, ROCHELLE

MRS. WALKER: Babysitter
MR. WALKER: Bank detective

Mr. Walker: I do criminal investigations for a bank. I was in the military police when I was in service. So police work was nothing new to me. My work is interesting. It's a little bit safer than being a city policeman. Very seldom do you come in contact with a shootout or anything of that nature. As far as I'm concerned, I'm going to stay in this job. But if something happened and I had to change jobs, I wouldn't be reluctant about changing. Because I feel whatever I go into I can accomplish or excel in it.

Mrs. Walker: I work at home, taking care of children in my home. I'm licensed in day care. I enjoy taking care of kids for right now. But I plan to get me a full-time job next year. 'Cause then my son will be going to school all day. I would like to take up an office job. In a nice office where I could meet a lot of people.

Mr. Walker: My father was a truck driver. I grew up on the South Side of Chicago. There was seven of us. And we were basically poor. But it wasn't destitute or anything like that. We had a good life. I brought my wife here with me from Cheyenne. I was in the service there. That's where I met her and where we got married.

We moved to this part of Chicago because this was one of the available apartments in the projects at the time. And since then I've been able to afford to move, but I don't want to. I like it here.

Mrs. Walker: I really feel unsafe, because I'm afraid to go out at night. Just to go to the store, I'm afraid. That's because of certain incidents that go around here. And certain things like robbing that happen.

Mr. Walker: Of course, there is more crime. I find myself watching where I go and what I do. That way I stay out of trouble. So I leave the nuts to themselves.

Mrs. Walker: I was born in Kansas City. After my mother died I lived with my sister in Lincoln, Nebraska. And then from there we moved to Cheyenne. I was around fifteen years old.

Mr. Walker: We're basically constituted as a black family. First of all, because I am black and head of the household. And I think that basically my ideals prevail, more or less. My son would ask me is he black or white. I tell him he is white because his complexion is white. And that his mommy is white. I also tell him, "Your sister is black and I'm black." That's the way it is. I want him to be aware of exactly what's going on. I want him to know the good and bad points of the black community, good and bad points of the white community too. And then he can decide for himself, because he certainly has a choice. My daughter, she doesn't have a choice.

I can remember, when I was young, there was a girl in school. Her skin was white and her father was black. And she like killed herself trying to convince everyone that she was black. And that's the wrong way to go. If they want to say you're white, then accept it for that. Be it good or bad, you know. You're going to have to put up with it.

THREE WISHES:
Mrs. Walker: To have a house. It would be in the suburbs. I'd like it where it's peaceful and quiet. Where no one is next to me on either side. Just a house where there's just me and my family. And a big yard where my kids could go out and run around. And like I said, I want to get me a really good job.

ABOUT THE PHOTOGRAPH:
Mr. Walker: It's very realistic. I like the composition of it. And like you say, the other photograph being in there makes it different.

Mrs. Walker: The other picture was taken at Sears. About a year ago. I wanted to have a big picture of my son, since I had a big picture of my daughter from school.

MARY AND DARBY HOLMES
CHILD: JESSE

MRS. HOLMES: Editor, educational publisher
MR. HOLMES: Jewelrymaker

Mrs. Holmes: Since I was sixteen, I've always worked. I took off six months when Jesse was born, knowing I'd go back. I'm incompetent at being a housewife. I just don't know how to do it. I work in educational publishing, and I write textbooks and throw together little activity kits and things like that. I'm ambitious. It's the right place for me to be right now.

Growing up in Wausau, Wisconsin, was real dull. Small town. Nothing much happened. My dad was a beer distributor. Middle-class family. Everything was extremely comfortable and secure. I didn't know at the time, but I had to leave Wausau and I did. I guess I needed to be in the city, where there is some action. I first left to go to the University of Wisconsin, and eventually came here to get a job. The friends I had in Wausau have all left. Not all of them have gone far. My brothers and sisters have left home, but they're in the same kind of towns, fifty miles away from Wausau.

Mr. Holmes: I'm trying real hard to make a living. Mary's been pretty much the support of the family. I'm just trying to find ways that allow me to do my jewelry work and sell enough of it so that I can keep on doing it. I enjoy dealing with people and selling them something that I've created entirely. It gives me a lot of satisfaction.

I was raised on the South Side, and I lived there until I was in my twenties. The South Side was the working folk: Polish, Irish workers, sort of upper lower-class, that kind of environment. My father was a cop. After I started working I ran into a lot of interesting people and it turned out that they all lived on the North Side. So I moved north when I got married. I like it a whole lot better here.

Question: Did you turn out the way your parents intended you to?

Mrs. Holmes: Oh, no. I should be somewhere in Wisconsin with about five kids. I would have gone to college, worked a few years, and married somebody respectable, and the way I was brought up that could be a social worker or a teacher. My family doesn't understand how Darby and I live at all. You know, that we live in a house that's one hundred years old, that it looks like this, that we live in a lot that is twenty-five feet wide. That just breaks them up.

Mr. Holmes: It's kind of hard to say. I don't think I really got any pressure from anybody to be anything. If I had had peer-group pressure, I would have turned out to be a burglar or car thief, because my friends turned out to be burglars, car thieves, and murderers. Frank is the only one out of the whole bunch that turned into a cop. They went off in directions that I just didn't, you know.

ABOUT THE CHILD:

Mrs. Holmes: I'm very ambitious for him. I mean I want Jesse to be the greatest Jesse that he can be. And I also think that he's got a lot of potential. And that's pretty ambitious.

Mr. Holmes: Probably the only hope that I have for him is that he'll get his act together and do what he wants to do. And just avoid some of the crap that I went through, in fact still am going through.

ABOUT THE PHOTOGRAPH:

Mrs. Holmes: I think the photograph shows that we're not a sweet little close-knit dependent family, but rather we are three quite different individuals who are comfortable with each other.

Mr. Holmes: If I was looking at this, I would probably think that these people were sort of semihippie types.

Mrs. Holmes: No. We look sort of semiprofessional types. *Hippie* is something different. And I think we look happy.

Mr. Holmes: With the exception of our son, who looks like a poor miserable little wretch.

Mrs. Holmes: We're positive, hard-working people, only slightly alienated!

PATRICIA AND THOMAS JAMES
CHILDREN: SARAH, SUSAN
DOG: KATY

MR. JAMES: Federal judge

Mrs. James: I had a very very happy childhood in Dundee, Scotland, even though it was during the war and my father died when I was only two.

About sixteen years ago, my sister and her husband were out in America—Springfield, Massachusetts. I made up my mind to visit them and to make my way all across America. And so I came out to see them with the intention of staying for a couple of years. After working there for sixteen months, I wanted to move further across America. I was going to go right over to the West Coast, but I arrived in Chicago, worked at the British Consulate, and met Tom here. So I didn't get any further across America.

When Tom and I became engaged, the last thing that we asked each other was where we wanted to live—because Tom was worried that I would say the suburbs, and I was worried that Tom would say the suburbs. But fortunately, we were both wrong. We have stayed in this neighborhood ever since.

Yes, I do feel different when I'm in Great Britain. I feel safer over there for sure. And there isn't the rudeness on the streets that there is over here, definitely. If people don't step aside, they're very apologetic that they haven't got out of your way. They say, "Thank you," if you open the door, whereas over here you can stand and hold the door open in a store and everybody just sails through and there's no "Thank you."

When I worked, I always worked as a secretary. I still like the excitement of getting down to the Loop. Some days when I take Sarah down to the orthodontist and we have a nine thirty appointment, we're hustling and bustling with the crowds and I think, "isn't this fun." But I wouldn't like it every day. Not again.

Mr. James: I suppose as I grew up I decided the suburbs were not the spot I wanted to be in. I had been born and raised in Evanston. Here in the city you live your life. You have an independence, and you do have a great deal of privacy. Even though we don't have twenty feet between each house, we do have more privacy here than I think you do in the suburbs.

I always had wanted to go to law school or business school. I was in the navy and had the GI Bill. So I applied to law school and was accepted and decided, yes, I'll go. I think probably in high school I was influenced by the Arthur Train stories about Mr. Tutt. They're stories about a lawyer—I can't remember now whether it's in New York or Boston—but he was a practitioner, an older gentleman who was very learned and sage. Anyway, law school was a happy choice. I enjoy my work. It's a great deal of challenge and a great deal of satisfaction.

THREE WISHES:
At my age you don't wish any more. Either you have to be happy or you had better change. I'm happy. I'm satisfied. If you wished, you would wish for doing things differently when you were younger. That's more a form of regret. I always wish I had spent more time on education when I was younger. Started off sooner and learned more. But as for whimsical wishes, I'd like to have a nice Peugeot, which to me is the finest automobile that has ever been made.

ABOUT THE PHOTOGRAPH:
Mrs. James: I love this photograph, I really do, but I'm sorry Glen, our other dog, isn't in it.

Mr. James: From the photograph, all that we could expect strangers to say about us is that we look happy. I don't think they could tell what we do for work or anything like that.

Mrs. James: The first time you photographed us, we were wondering what was just going to happen. The second time we decided let's get dressed for it and have a nice family picture, all together, all dressed up.

Mr. James: And if the girls are going to be in long dresses, I should be dressed too. And we enjoyed it!

GRACE AND COURTNEY BURRESS
CHILDREN: GLENDON, REGINA

MRS. BURRESS: Medical assistant
MR. BURRESS: Salesman for publishing company

Mr. Burress: It's that constant search for a place to live where you feel—I guess *safe* could be the word. We've lived on the West, South, and North sides of Chicago. And now we're about to move back south again to a suburb.

Mrs. Burress: I have mixed feelings about moving. I think it would be nice for the kids, you know, to be out of the city, but I'm afraid I might feel shut off from city life.

Mr. Burress: You see, I'm tired of the city. I'm tired of the hustle—the crowded things and the bars and burglar alarms and locks and things like that. And not trusting people. And you know, since I've taken a new job last year I traveled in about three states through all kinds of communities. And I got a chance to see people leaving doors open, everybody smiling at everybody. And I kind of want to do that.

I grew up in a housing project, Near West Side of Chicago. We were lower-lower class. My mother raised us. She worked and did the best she could, but we were always needing something. Always. I wouldn't want my kids to go through what I went through. I started off in night school while I was working. It was frustrating. And so I quit a couple of times. I took a job with the government as a clerk. Top-notch clerk I thought I was. But every time promotion time came they always found an excuse not to promote me. I finally realized that I had to get more education. So I went back to school at night. And then I got a scholarship to the University of Omaha.

I stayed a year in Omaha. While I was there I got fed up with basketball. You see, I was a history major and, in fact, the coach tried to persuade me to change my major to P.E. Because my books were costing too much money. All the other guys changed to P.E., but I wouldn't go for it. A lot of them dropped out. And the coach seemed like he didn't care. He had one thing on his mind, and that was a winning season. When I saw he was just out for himself, I became disillusioned with basketball. So I came home to Chicago and finished up at Chicago State. The coach there begged me to play basketball, but I wouldn't. I also changed my major from history to education.

I taught school for five years. I was doing everything, and I wasn't getting any rewards for it. My principal got credit, bonus points, for everything that I started, like gifted programs, basketball teams, counseling on the lunch hour. And the inequities of the school system came to me. They keep talking about inner feelings and good things you do for the kids. Yeah, that's great, but then when you think about your kids at home, that you want to do things for them, and you are trying not to live over your head. So I decided to leave teaching, and I started working for a publishing company.

ABOUT THE PHOTOGRAPH:

Mr. Burress: That's us right now, today.

Mrs. Burress: And by the pictures in the back they get another picture of us.

Mr. Burress: And strangers would probably judge from the trophies that I'm an athlete. A couple on the top shelf are my son's. He's slowly replacing me and he's pushing mine to the back of the shelf.

Question: Will strangers get the right impression of you from the photo?

Mr. Burress: Well, I had just come in from a day's work so I had on a suit and tie. So maybe people wouldn't get an accurate picture of me. Because normally I don't wear a suit and tie, except to work. If they took a look at our income, me in a shirt and a tie, a black family where the wife and the husband are in the same house together—they are going to say "Middle class. Bourgeois." But that would not be a true description of us. It takes two incomes for us to be lower-middle or middle or whatever society says we are, and we're struggling. And I still have my own roots in my old neighborhood, the projects, and I hope I never lose them.

Mrs. Burress: Like Courtney, I came from the projects. I came from a family of ten, six boys and four girls. And my mother did it by herself. And of course it was rough. I don't know how she did it. I didn't meet Courtney till high school, even though we lived three blocks from each other.

Right after high school I worked while Courtney was in school. So I didn't get to go to college. Finally in 1972 I took a course as a medical assistant. And that's what I am now. I work for a private physician in a clinic. And I do everything. Answer the phones, give injections, blood pressure, weights and stuff like that. I love it.

ABOUT THE CHILDREN:
Mrs. Burress: I want them to have an education and to be happy.

Mr. Burress: One of the reasons that we want to change communities is, I want their peers to have the same kind of ideas that they have. You see, the neighborhood that we came from, there were no pressures to do well in school. My pressures came from within. Because I wanted things to be better for me than they were for my father and mother. I also wanted to be qualified, so that if I didn't like my job I could leave and go somewhere else. I wouldn't have to beg.

If my children want to go to college, I'll be more than happy. I'll be elated. If they don't, I'll be disappointed, but I don't want to force them. Being black, there are a lot of doors closed. And I want them to be prepared so that when the doors open—and they're opening all the time—I want them to be able to step in.

I go back to my old neighborhood often. I feel my roots are there. Most of our old friends are on dope. Most of them are unemployed. A lot of them are even dead now. Overdoses. Or dead from hurting one another. But certain friends are going to be your friends no matter what. You know, I still drink out of the same bottle.

Mrs. Burress: I don't go into the neighborhood. My mother still lives there, but I normally don't go over there. And I really don't like the idea of him going over there. But all his friends are over there. I have this fear, you know. Once you live over there it doesn't seem so bad, when you're part of the community. But I'm out of it now and I just don't feel relaxed over there.

Mr. Burress: When I go back there I don't pretend that I'm better than they are. And we don't talk about the things I've managed to do. We just talk about what everybody's doing, what's happening, the Ali-Frazier fight. Or mainly, I play ball over there. Like this summer I was over there every day exercising.

Statistics released show that the average black living in one of those ghetto kind of conditions is fifteen times more likely to die from a homicide than a white person coming from another environment. So you know, that's why I want to create something different for the kids and for Grace. So that they can have a better chance. For myself, I could go back there and live. I never wanted to work for a lot of money. I don't need much for myself. But I feel like I have an obligation now.

JEAN AND JOHN ENTWISTLE
CHILDREN: DANIEL, JOHN

MRS. ENTWISTLE: University administrator
MR. ENTWISTLE: Corporate executive

Mr. Entwistle: We came to Lincoln Park eight years ago.

Mrs. Entwistle: We think it's a wonderful place to live, very close to the center of town, very close to the art galleries, which are my special love. It would be hard to find a place that would be for us handier.

Mr. Entwistle: It's first and primarily the people in our neighborhood that give us a sense of community. Here there are people that share our interests and mores. We have property interests and law interests and interests in getting the garbage collected and interests in keeping crime away. And it isn't a situation where you anticipate everybody's going to move away.

Mrs. Entwistle: It's very stable.

Mr. Entwistle: It's very stable because many of the people own their own properties. As an example, these townhouses were built in 1968, and not one has turned over.

Mrs. Entwistle: The homeowners know each other. Because the property is expensive, it requires a constant investment of yourself to keep it up. And there are great conversations up and down the block about which grass seed is best and where to get geraniums.

There has been tremendous upgrading in the neighborhood; the properties have had a load of money poured into them. In some ways that's sad, because it means that people who may have been happy to have made their home here no longer can afford to do so. And that is a limiting thing, and in some respects that can be a little boring. I find the boring comes from the sameness of age. You'd like to see older people around here, and there are very few older people.

Mr. Entwistle: I was raised in a very nice city neighborhood in Trenton, New Jersey. Of course when I was a boy you didn't have the phenomenon of recently built suburbs that you have now. So my city neighborhood was probably analogous with today's suburb. My father was a fireman. And although firemen have never broken records for making money, in the thirties they had jobs, and therefore were relatively quite well off. Trenton wasn't a terribly stimulating environment to grow up in. It was a comfortable environment which had pluses and minuses.

Mrs. Entwistle: I grew up in the same town as did Jay, although I didn't know him until one year before our marriage. I recall it in pretty much the same manner, except that I constantly thought that it was very dull—and probably developed my affinity to live in big cities because of living in a place like that. There was no neighborhood spirit, and everyone was a self-sufficient unit. And they came and went in their automobiles. And so you never knew your neighbors really, and there wasn't the kind of neighborliness that there is here.

Mr. Entwistle: My parents were fairly ambitious for me, I think. They're dead now, but I think how I turned out would amaze them. I wasn't known as an early bloomer. But I seemed to have accomplished more, I would say, than maybe most of the kids with whom I grew up.

I am an executive for a large American company, and I'm in what they call the operations end of the business. My job is very important to me. I get a lot of pleasure out of it and a lot of identity out of it.

Mrs. Entwistle: I've had several jobs, but mostly always in education. Educational administration is my particular interest right now. I'm currently working at a major university in a center which is an academic "think tank," helping to plan the projects that will be gone into and funded. I also serve as an executive assistant to one of the vice presidents of the university. My work is very important to me. I am constantly thinking, How can I get a better position which would indicate that I am ambitious? Which is why I prefer a big-city atmosphere. It makes all these things more possible.

Question: Can you put yourselves in a class?

Mr. Entwistle: Well, I think in this country we tend to define ourselves economically versus background or whatever. So I'd say maybe upper-middle-class. However, I know some people who by virtue of their own income might not be a member of, say, the middle class, but because their parents had funds and they went to certain schools and had a certain background, they, in fact, are able to maintain a firm. But I think at the bottom of it, the American society tends to classify people economically. We lived in Europe for a year and I think there the difficulty of changing class, if you will, is substantially greater than it is in America.

Older Child: I think it's education and money. Because any dope can have a fortune, but that doesn't make him rich or high-class.

ABOUT THE CHILDREN:

Mr. Entwistle: I am very ambitious for the children, very ambitious for them, but not in a narrowly defined way. I mean I am not terrible anxious as to whether they are materially successful. I think it serves one very well to have material success. But beyond that I think that a person should be able to say at the middle and at the end of what they're doing that they like it, and that it satisfies them and fulfills them. And whatever way they work that out is a function of things that I don't know how to calculate. I only know how to do it myself, but I can't get into someone else's skin and tell them. And I think it's extremely important that people are useful and do things that challenge and develop them, hopefully to the benefit of persons other than themselves.

Mrs. Entwistle: I very much hope they will grow up to lead the kind of lives that we will be proud of in the future, that they will hold to the ideals that we have tried to give them, so that they'll be loyal to the vows that they make to employers, to their spouses, to their children. And they will take their place in the community as "people of some count," as they used to say in the old days. And that doesn't neces-sarily have to be the kind of thing that makes front-page headlines.

THREE WISHES:

Older Child: One, a free certificate for every comic book that comes into Brown's Drugstore. Two, for a truckload of gold, to get in the gold business. And three would probably be to stay in the school that I am in until I graduate from college. I've got one more wish. I'd like to have a permit and a machine gun. The permit would say that I could shoot down every single blasted cigarette package and sign advertising them.

ABOUT THE PHOTOGRAPH:

Mr. Entwistle: I think it's a good representative picture of all of us in our home setting. It may even show our personalities a bit.

Mrs. Entwistle: I like John's face here very much, because here you see the budding adolescent coming out there.

Older Child: Yeah, I think that this tells you something. 'Cause if you were looking at that picture or I was, I'd probably think, hey, these people live fairly well. All that art and everything. And I'd think they're rather old-fashioned with that piece there.

MARY AND RAY PREDENKIEWICZ

MRS. PREDENKIEWICZ: Pharmacist
MR. PREDENKIEWICZ: Construction superintendent

Mr. Predenkiewicz: My mother's parents came from Poland. My father's parents were born in this country, but their parents were born in Poland, too. My own father was a repairman for International Harvester. Worked for them for thirty-some-odd years and he retired from there.

We were very poor. We lived in a neighborhood in Chicago that was Polish and Slavic. Grandmother spoke Polish, and I could understand it and speak a few words when I was like twelve or thirteen, but other than that I really can't say that I had a Polish upbringing. I could talk about family values.

Mrs. Predenkiewicz: A lot of clichés, like, "You never get anything for nothing." "No matter what you earn, put something aside."

Mr. Predenkiewicz: Or a typical one: "You're not wasting money if you eat it."

Mrs. Predenkiewicz: My family was probably better off, maybe lower-middle-class. My father was a grocer. Both he and my mother worked in the grocery store. A very religious house, and you came out of it with all kinds of guilt feelings afterwards. Ray says to me, "Don't go to church. Go to your mother's."

Mr. Predenkiewicz: We moved out of the neighborhood many years ago. You see, in ethnic neighborhoods you don't find any young people. Our lives now are completely different and we could probably never go back to live.

We moved here five years ago because I liked the neighborhood and I liked the houses. We took a house that will be one hundred years old next year, and we completely renovated it. We thought we were going to live here all our lives, but we have just sold it, and we are taking off.

You see, I always wanted to take off for a year between our tenth and eleventh year of marriage. After about ten years all the stuff that you have is garbage. The towels that you had when you were first married, they're worn out. O.K. The toaster breaks. If you notice, we have no furniture right now. At one time we had a whole houseful. And it just went to hell.

We're going to Florida for a while, and then we're going to travel in Europe, and then when we come back we're going to hit the salmon run in Oregon. In September we'll worry about where we're going to settle down.

I think what we're about to do is exciting. Because we chose it. We didn't have to sell the house. But I am a little frightened. We don't really know what we're going to run into, and we have never done anything like this before.

Mrs. Predenkiewicz: I think that in a way, having a house and everything is security. By the same token, not having it is freedom. I don't know what all this is going to bring. I may get lonely the second week away and look into windows and envy other ladies fixing dinner or something. But we have to try it.

Mr. Predenkiewicz: I really believe like in this country today, that if you wanted to be a millionaire you still could, if you wanted to give up everything. But there are really too many nice things in the world to do than chase the dollar.

ABOUT THE PHOTOGRAPH:

Mr. Predenkiewicz: I haven't the slightest idea what strangers would think.

Mrs. Predenkiewicz: They would think, "What's that old man doing with such a young girl!"

Mr. Predenkiewicz: They might think we're just ordinary people.

Mrs. Predenkiewicz: If I didn't know us, I would like that picture. We look friendly and happy.

Mr. Predenkiewicz: It's really hard to say. I think that picture's like me. I really do. I think it's like Mary, too. She's sort of looking out of the side of her eyes. She's somewhat standoffish, and it looks like that.

SUSAN AND WARREN THUNDER
CHILDREN: WARREN JR., LINDA

MRS. THUNDER: Office clerk
MR. THUNDER: Lathe operator

Mrs. Thunder: My husband grew up in Wisconsin. Yes, he's Indian. Menominee. I grew up here, just a couple of blocks away. We want to move out to the country. Someplace. Everything is changing. Well, I guess it's changing all over, but I don't know. Just everybody, you know, getting killed and everything. We're going to try to move up to Wisconsin within a couple of years. I just started working now so we can save money to go up there. I'm doing office work, production clerk. We've been visiting up there in Wisconsin a lot. See, he has relatives up there, so we go visit regularly. We like it up there.

When we go up there we go up for Indian dances and stuff. And my daughter's already learning how to dance and that. And when my son gets older he'll learn how, too. My husband didn't really learn the language when he was younger, but his mother and father know it. They just didn't pass it on. I don't know why. But he knows some words. Since knowing him I've learned a lot more about Indians and that.

THREE WISHES:
Mrs. Thunder: A house, I guess. Our own house. Just to have a happy life, you know. Not see any of my kids get sick or die or anything.
Mr. Thunder: To be in Wisconsin. All three of my wishes.
Mrs. Thunder: My husband's not really a shy person once you know him. I mean, he's a lot more outgoing than I am. Once he starts talking you can't get him to stop either. I guess with people he doesn't know, he doesn't like to talk.

ABOUT THE PHOTOGRAPH:
Mrs. Thunder: This picture just shows us the way we are naturally. That's us.

CAROLYN WIESE

CHILD: JOANNA

MRS. WIESE: School teacher

I came to Chicago four years ago from Houston. I had worked here for a year after college, so I knew the city and I knew that we could survive here. I also knew that no matter where in the city I got a job, I could get there on city transportation. You see, I don't drive.

I grew up in a small town in Missouri. People had chickens, you know, behind the house and gardens. Sort of half-rural. My father had come from Tennessee. His job was to map out levees on the Missouri River to prevent flooding. That's what he did all his life. Because he had only a high school education, he could never advance. So an education was important to him. That's one reason that he saw to it we were educated. My mother came from Georgia.

Many of our relatives lived in Tennessee, but I didn't know any of them really. Our immediate family was just a little group of people all by ourselves. I have three or four aunts and six cousins and I've never seen any of them. And my grandparents lived into their eighties, and I think I saw them only once. They were hillbillies, lived in the hill country of Tennessee. I think my mother started quite early with the idea that she wanted us to go to school. And she knew that in order for us to do that, it was better if we didn't associate too closely with people who did not have the same thing in mind. Right or wrong, she accomplished this by isolating us from people. Like we didn't entertain, we didn't have people come over.

For this reason I find that, as an adult, I am more or less content to be by myself. And I really mean that. Because I've tried the thing of being gregarious and all that. But I found that most of the things that I choose to do for relaxation are things that I do alone—like reading and sewing and playing musical instruments—and I'm quite happy doing them.

As children we had a great deal of privacy that children don't have today. I think this is the thing, the biggest thing missing from children's lives now. The right to go off by yourself without mother, and just think and be by yourself. Today people feel a compulsion to introduce children to every thing—to take them dancing and Scouts and baton-twirling. And you know, it's nice, but it winds up that they're always with adults and they're always receiving instructions. I mean there's a type of creativity that you ruin with all this.

Question: Can you put yourself in a class?

In other words, I feel certain things in common with very ordinary people, and I also feel certain things in common with very well educated people. It creates somewhat of a dilemma. When you teach, you don't get wealthy and you don't associate with what they'd call upper-middle-class people, because you really can't afford the activities. Like I don't find myself greatly involved with people, for instance, who go sailing or travel a great deal. And yet you can enjoy these people because of their education. At the same time there can be a lot of pretenses and I'm not comfortable with them. For that reason, I find sometimes I'm more comfortable with very ordinary people. So I guess you can become very well educated in our society, but you can only advance as far as your money is going to let you.

ABOUT THE PHOTOGRAPH:

Joanna is a very friendly little child, and that doesn't show in the photograph you've chosen. As for me, I don't think that much of what I am really surfaces. In other words, I sort of present a blank face. I've looked around at people who've taught for a hundred years, and part of the conditioning you go through is that you're constantly failing to react to things. And that is because the children like to test you all day. So what you learn to do is ignore it, and just more or less show no expression. I think it becomes part of your personality, which is rather tragic.

ANNETTE AND BILL CAMPBELL

MRS. CAMPBELL: Planner, government commission
MR. CAMPBELL: Public relations worker, government agency

Mrs. Campbell: This part of Chicago is fashionable. Most people move here the first time that they leave their family nucleus. So they're out here looking for fun, excitement, looking for a partner. And all of that is not conducive to a sense of neighborhood.

Mr. Campbell: We dig checking out the neighborhood, you know, just going for walks and seeing people. But some people are super uptight about the black people in this area. You know, like if I'm out by myself and I'm walking, I encounter people on the street who are really uptight by the fact that I am walking down the sidewalk with them. And that makes me upset. And you know, I see tactical unit cars of the police department just kind of following me, a half a block behind me, and that kind of thing. It kind of makes a strong feeling of alienation. And like wow, it makes me uncomfortable.

Mrs. Campbell: I don't think there's an openness to a more substantial black population. Most of the whites that we know up here feel comfortable now. And that's because minority groups are just that, minority groups, in this community.

Mr. Campbell: People here for the most part are very compartmentalized. You know, they get out of their car and walk into the building and come up the elevator and go into their apartment. Like whatever lies beyond their apartment doors is their life. And they feel, you know, no need in speaking. I'm a very outgoing type of person, and I speak to folks. And you know, it's a very jarring thing for me when people don't respond in a warm fashion.

Mrs. Campbell: My parents always stressed that you should be independent and not hinge on what other people think about you or whether they're warm or cold. So I suppose it was a good preparation for this type of environment now. I grew up on the South Side of Chicago. My mother is a housewife. My father's a basketball and football official as well as an independent businessman now. They continue to move up along the economic strata.

Question: Can you put your family into a class?

Mrs. Campbell: I have problems putting people in a class. But I suppose my family is solidly middle-class in thinking and in their way of life and economically. I suppose on a black family scale they are upper-middle-class or upper-class blacks. But compared to the white American norm, I would say they are middle-class.

Mr. Campbell: Both our fathers attained college degrees and moved up into the business world. My father is in a corporation. He started out as a chemist and worked his way to vice president of the company. And everyone is expected to go to college, get their degree, and go out and make it.

But being a black family there are certain limitations which you might hit. And I think for both me and Annette those limitations are more words than they are reality. As we look at our friends, their basic ambitions and goals are to have kids, to have a nice house, and to have a job which is very secure, and just drop into that niche. And I think we both realize that where we plan to go in our lives might differ from those folks we've grown up with.

Mrs. Campbell: I suppose we're striving more towards a universal consciousness, something deeper, something more basic.

ABOUT THE PHOTOGRAPH:

Mr. Campbell: The room is kind of an extension of us. That's why I dig it. Like the picture in the background on the left is one my mother painted from a picture she saw in *National Geographic.*

Mrs. Campbell: I'm really pleased with the photograph. It has so many of the things that are a part of us in it. It looks like something we would have had commissioned.

DOROTHY AND HIROSHI KANEKO
MASANO AND MOTOTSUGU MORITA
(Mrs. Kaneko's parents)
CHILD: KEVIN
DOG: KIPPY

MRS. KANEKO: Group worker
MR. KANEKO: Carpenter

Mr. Morita: My grandpa was a Samurai. My father was a farmer, and then he came to United States. And then after he come over here he called me. So I came here 1911. My father started to farm in Oregon, fruit farm. And because the war started, all the Japanese had to evacuate from the West Coast. We had to go into camps, first in California and then to a camp in Idaho. After 1944, after the peace, you go back free any place. I thought I would go back into farming, but my youngsters—you know I have nine children—they like to stay here in Chicago. They wanted to try a new life here. That's why we settled here in 1945.

We went back to visit Japan in 1960. After the war everything changed. In the city they like modern styles just like in the United States. Modern buildings so high up. "Oh," I thought, "It looks just like America." But in the country, maybe here and there you find old-style Japanese houses. But there are very few left.

I'm eighty-two years old. I try not to worry. Always look for the bright side, you know. Forget about dark side. Of course you got to watch what you eat. Vegetables and fish. I don't eat too much meat. You got to take care of yourself. . . . You know, I have twenty-one grandchildren, and two great-grandchildren.

Mrs. Kaneko: My parents are very helpful in the fact that they clean house for me, they do the cooking, they take care of my yard. They also go every Wednesday to clean my brother's office. He's a dentist. I think it's good for them too. They feel like they have some responsibility and a job.

I'm considered a group worker at the Japanese-American Service Committee. We have about one hundred elderly people there; the average age is seventy-six. My main activity is to arrange for all sorts of activities. You know, my generation are very appreciative of our senior citizens, because they're the ones that came over here and worked so hard to make a home for us here. We second-generation and third-generation are very concerned about the Issei, or the first generation. And we'll do almost anything for them. And that's mainly what my work is concerned with; the Issei.

Mr. Kaneko: I was born in a little mining town in Oregon. My dad first went there as a type of stationary engineer, taking care of pumping the water out from the mineshaft. Around 1920 or so we all went to Japan for a visit. And it so happened that I guess it was kind of hard for them to make a living with us three children, so when I was about twelve or thirteen they left us in Japan with our grandparents. And then they came back to farm in Oregon. In the meantime we grew up in Japan until I came back to the United States in 1930.

ABOUT THE PHOTOGRAPH:

Mr. Morita: When I went to Japan to visit and had to sit down on the mat like that, I sure had a hard time. It hurts! It hurts, so you go sideways.

Mrs. Kaneko: The photograph looks like Japan rather than Chicago.

Mr. Kaneko: I guess it's a good description of our family. But a couple of the girls are missing. And of course these are my wife's parents rather than my own.

Mrs. Kaneko: What he means is in Japan usually the eldest son would be more or less looking after his parents. He's the eldest son, but these are *my* parents.

Mr. Kaneko: According to Japanese custom, the oldest son had to take care of the parents. I mean, that was their duty and responsibility. And, well, that kind of creates a little atmosphere that I would say is for the betterment of everyone, because you just don't do the thing that you sometimes want to in front of a parent. And, well, that's why I think the crime among the Orientals is very small. Because they have this family tie.

Question: How do you happen to be in Chicago?

Mr. Kaneko: We got married in Oregon in 1942 before we went to this camp. We called it a relocation camp. Well, actually it was more or less a concentration camp, because it had a barbed wire fence and we couldn't get out and there were guards all around it. We stayed there one year. You could get out of the camp if you had a job. The government paid the fare to whatever place you wanted to go.

Mrs. Kaneko: As long as you didn't go to the West Coast . . .

Mr. Kaneko: And so we looked for a job around this part of the country.

Mrs. Kaneko: I got a domestic job in Barrington. And then we were assured a place to live. After a while I was expecting, so we couldn't stay there. And we came to the city, to Chicago.

Question: How Japanese do you feel?

Mr. Kaneko: Before the war we felt we were second-class citizens. We rejected everything that was Japanese because we wanted to be part of America as much as possible.

Mrs. Kaneko: It was sometime after the war that we began to appreciate our own culture. I wasn't familiar with it too much, except from what I learned from my parents. And then I began to think maybe there's something here. When I went to Japan I was sure of it. And then our girls went to Japan, the first in 1963 for Junior Year Abroad. They really appreciated the Japanese culture and they learned to speak Japanese. One of our daughters now lives in Japan. She married a Japanese student who was studying over here. My son doesn't yet seem to have an interest in going to Japan, but he listens and communicates with my parents and I think that's a little progress. I'm hoping one day he'll say, "I want to take Japanese lessons."

ARLENE AND CARLOS PALOMAR
CHILDREN: MARIA, LEONARD, DAVID
GRANDCHILD: FERNANDO CARLOS VELEZ

MRS. PALOMAR: Teacher aide
MR. PALOMAR: Insurance agent

Mr. Palomar: My parents brought me from Texas as a child here. And I grew up in Chicago. My family is from Mexico. Their customs were customs of their land. And I was brought up under those same customs. And I'm very very much Americanized now, you know. We didn't teach our kids Spanish, because we hardly speak it here. But as your children get older, of course they recognize the culture. They become very much aware of it. Whereas years back, when I was a teenager, no. Then you didn't want to shout out, "Hey, I'm a Mexican-American. And if you don't like it, too bad."

When I was growing up it was the fact that if you were an Anglo—great. That's where it was at. Mexican-American? Well, you're not really black, but you're in-between. And I was made very much aware of this because when I was in grammar school, if you recall, they have you write an autobiography of yourself. I put down, "Well, O.K. I'm Charlie Palomar, blah, blah, and I'm white." Well, of course, I wasn't black, so I was led to believe I'm white. So when I got my autobiography back, my teacher corrected me. She said, "No, you're not a white. You're brown." So all of a sudden my world completely collapsed around me, you know.

All the second-generation people, if you were to talk to them, they all experienced the same thing I've experienced. Well now, these kids are beginning to appreciate the culture. Because all the homework's been done for them already. So they come, "Hey, I'm a Mexican-American." Beautiful, you know. Beautiful. That's right and proud of it. The pride is that they can walk down the street with their head up. And they don't step back to anybody. I want them to feel that they're just as good as you are. And I

don't care who you are. Because my dad told me when I was growing up, he says, "Listen, they don't respect you for who you are. They respect you for the amount of education you have."

One day I took my three kids to the lake front when they were younger, and we saw the big yachts. You know, along the yacht basin up there. And one of my little boys asked me, he says, "Hey, why can't we afford a boat like that?" And I says, "When you get older, you become a professional man. And then you'll be able to afford a boat like that." So I explained to them that what would get him these material things would be education. And if I have to work harder, I'm going to do it because I want them to have this education. I'd like them to go into maybe medicine, or law, or accounting. Something that they'll be paid for what they know and not too much what they can do.

I'm an insurance agent. I was a prelaw student. I dropped out of college because I got emotionally involved. And so I went into the service. I wish I had never quit school. There's a lot of Latin-American attorneys. But there has never been a good criminal Latin-American attorney. And that was my goal. I was going to be the best Latin-American criminal attorney in the city of Chicago.

Mrs. Palomar: My father was from a small town right outside of San Antonio, and my mother was from Houston. She was very young when she came here and so was my father. I guess my father probably did the same thing my husband's father did—worked in the coal mines. My father's parents were from Mexico. It is just a coincidence that my father's family knew my husband's father in Texas.

We've been in this neighborhood for thirteen years. The thirteen years we've been here, you know, we've never had any trouble. But I will admit that I'm afraid to walk down the street. But I'm just that way. I won't drive, I won't go out at night either. And I find that the older I'm getting, the worse it's getting.

The neighborhood is changing. All your families are leaving. What you got here is singles. We've felt it at school too. Because enrollment has gone down. I'm a teacher aide. I took the teacher aide exam while I was a school community rep, and I've been a teacher aide for four years now. It's a nice job, but I don't think I would like to keep doing it all the time. The ideal job? Well, I probably would have been a housewife. But once you get a taste of the extra money . . . This is the thing, you know, that made me start working. Otherwise I probably would have gotten used to staying home and doing things that I like to do. And do them right. And keep things nice and neat.

THREE WISHES:

Mrs. Palomar: We were playing the lottery, and I was just wishing we could win it and I could stay home. That would be more than enough money for the three kids to get a good education. And probably take a trip to Mexico, which we've been planning to do for I don't know how long. And then I guess I would get myself a new car.

ABOUT THE PHOTOGRAPH:

Mr. Palomar: The first time you came I think everybody was a little uptight about it, you know. I think by coming back a second time, you got a more candid picture.

Mrs. Palomar: Yes, the second time the kids were just their normal selves. Leonard and Maria were really against dressing up. This is the way they like to be. Comfortable.

LYNNE GLASER
CHILDREN: JASON, DAWN

MS. GLASER: Administrative assistant, special school

I've hung around this neighborhood since I was fifteen years old. And I went to school at DePaul University, which is down here. I really love this neighborhood. Living here was planned like from Day One that I split from my husband. And I worked my ass off to get here, managing my finances and all that. It was just everything I would want for my kids—the public school is Number Two or Three in the city, and St. Vincent's is one of the best day care centers in the city, if not the country. And everything I could want for me really is here. Just the people in the neighborhood. Great.

I was born in Chicago and raised here, but I went to school in the suburbs. My family was middle-class, striving to be upper-middle-class, second-generation Jewish family. I'm third-generation. My dad now works for the Democratic machine. I'm not sure what his title is. He didn't always work for the machine, but he always wanted to.

I worked for a brief period at a bank, and I was making a great amount of money. But the working conditions for me there were terrible, and I didn't like the way I was being treated, and one day I woke up crying and I said, "That's it." And I quit. Then several months later I happened to see a job in the paper, the kind of thing I knew I wanted to do. It was learning administrative procedures and writing proposals for a school for emotionally disturbed children. I lucked out and got the job. I'm learning a real lot and everybody that works there is extremely dedicated and intelligent. In the past few months I've just developed as a person and have gotten more confidence in myself than I have had in years.

ABOUT THE CHILDREN:

I want them to be good. I don't want to see them get into all sorts of trouble or wanting to drop out of school or getting into trouble with the law. I want them to be able to learn things. That's the basic thing. I want them to want knowledge about things. College for me was fun and games, a big play house. It's not until now that I realized everything that I missed. I went to college for a year and a half and then I got married.

In ten years' time? I do hope in ten years' time I have my college degree. And all the confidence I need to be happy. I suspect I'll be remarried by then. I don't really want to spend all my life by myself. But that's another thing. I want to first be independent. I also mean totally confident when I say independent. I want to have the freedom to do whatever I want and to know or think whatever I'm saying is right.

Question: How do you feel about being in a book?

I thought, be in a book, let other people see you. It's a neat thing. It's cool.

The people in your book probably all have certain personality traits that are similar in the respect that they've allowed themselves to come out. O.K. They're probably more open people, more giving people, and they have nothing to hide. Maybe they've had better experiences in their lives. I always think about that a lot, because you know, especially living in a big city, there's a lot of crime in this area. And people get worried about outsiders coming in and knowing where you live and what your habits are. So I guess, depending on what kind of experiences you've had, they might not be as open as other people.

ABOUT THE PHOTOGRAPH:

This photograph seems to reflect their personalities. I seem to have the biggest smile, and Dawn looks like Dawn and Jason looks like Jason. Jason's mouth on my breast may be saying something, I don't know! I have a difficult time perceiving myself in pictures anyway. It's a blank. Usually I can never decide if it's me or not.

MARIA AND ALFREDO ACIERTO
(parents of Mary Ridley)

MRS. ACIERTO: School teacher
MR. ACIERTO: Retired Post Office worker

Mr. Acierto: I came from the Philippines in 1924. I wanted to get some education, you know. And love of adventure. All those things. I heard that in Chicago you got lots of opportunities for education and work. And I had my relatives over here. My uncles. That's why I came over here.

In the Philippines, my father was a merchant. He sold some things like coconuts. Bought them in one place and sold them in another. We had two boats, sailboats.

When I came here I worked in the U.S. Post Office, and at the same time went to school. I finished my high school and my college education over here. I worked in the Post Office until I retired. Then I worked in a bank.

I was in the service in World War II. From Japan we stopped in the Philippines, where I met my wife. I got married. Right there.

Now I'm retired. I got lots of things to do, like, for instance, taking care of my plants, taking care of the buildings, one building over here and one over by Jim and Mary. I go there everyday and see to it that everything is in good shape. And I water my plants over there. I sometimes go there and shovel the snow. I work for pleasure now, you see. If I don't want to go, I don't have to go over.

Mrs. Acierto: I came to Chicago in 1946. Yes, I was married in the Philippines before I came here. I think the best place is still Chicago. I like it here, and, you know, the children are here. We have three grown children, one girl and two boys.

We love to travel. Now we have not only stayed in Spain, but we have traveled all the way to Israel and to Africa, as far as Marrakesh, you know. And I certainly have seen a lot of the West Coast, too. Both of us went to Mexico last July and we're going to go again next summer. Since 1969 we went to the Philippine Islands, and from there we stopped in Japan and then, of course we have gone to England because Mary, my daughter, married an Englishman. The parents of Jim, her husband, are so nice I think they have some kind of a feeling, like you know, like we are all Filipinos.

I teach in a high school. I teach Spanish and I have worked at the Board of Education as a writer for the curriculum guide. I can say that it is a difficult school, but I have never had any trouble with those kids. No. We have all kinds. We have fourteen different ethnic groups. I have sponsored an International Club since 1967, and there are a lot of black, brown, Polack, yellow, Italian, all kinds, white. And we have a nice time. If you respect the kids and know what you're doing there's no reason to have trouble.

THREE WISHES:
I want to travel around the world. He wants to go to Africa and I'd like to go with him. And I want to go to South America. And, well, knock on wood, both of us ought to be healthy, you know. If we could continue all those things that we have, that would be very nice. And to just keep our kids together.

You know, we had talked among ourselves about buying a house together—all of the kids and their families. And we have bought a home about a mile from here. They are living there now, and we're thinking of moving there too.

MARY AND JIM RIDLEY
CHILD: EMILY

MRS. RIDLEY: School teacher
MR. RIDLEY: Architect

Mrs. Ridley: I was born at sea, on the way to the States from the Philippines. I've spent practically all my life in Chicago, except for the year I was in England. My family are all very close. When I was a child my two brothers and me, plus three of our cousins, lived all together in the same house where my parents are living now. It was very close-knit. And we stayed close all through high school and even when I was in college. I think a close family is a very typically Filipino thing.

Mr. Ridley: It's like every friend of Mary's parents that comes to the house is auntie or uncle, you know, regardless of whether they're relations. It's hard to tell who is family and who isn't because everyone is welcome.

Mrs. Ridley: Yes, we have a very large extended-family kind of thing which encompasses people who really aren't related. Jim and I are still very involved with my family. We bought this building and the one next door as a family thing. And two of my brothers are living in apartments next door.

I thought surely Jim would miss England a lot more, be a lot more homesick. And I was really rather surprised that he took to living in Chicago much better than I took to living in England.

Mr. Ridley: I miss England about as much as I expected to. Really, I would like to spend more time in England, but it's just not possible. I'm quite happy to go back every two years. I like Chicago a lot. I don't feel misplaced at all.

I was born outside London at Wimbledon, which is a suburb. I went away to school starting when I was five years old, so, you know, a lot of time I spent away from home. And my brother and sister and I were just together on vacations. Well, looking back on it I would have much preferred not to have done that. It just wasn't very worthwhile.

My father is a chartered accountant. Now he's retired. I think the most important thing that he was concerned about was that we should all have some profession. He was brought up in the age when it was difficult to get jobs and, you know, you stayed in the job the whole of your life.

Well, all the time through school I sort of thought, "Well, I'll probably be a chartered accountant." And then I just decided it was the last thing I wanted to be. It was when I was doing a lot of art at school. And it just struck me one day that I could be an architect. So I went to see a careers officer at school. I must have been about sixteen. And he said I didn't stand a chance and said, "Why don't you be a shoe designer?" And "There's a lot of interest in wallpaper designers." But anyway I did get into architecture school and got through. I'm very happy with what I've chosen. Altogether I never thought I would have been so lucky.

Question: Can you put yourselves in a class?

Mrs. Ridley: We fit really well into the middle-class kind of situation, both here and in England. We both have a profession. I think class gets down to economics and what you make during a year. I mean if we were to put ourselves into a bag, that's the one I think we fit into.

Mr. Ridley: I think there's a lot more to it. In England, class is something that's very traditional. The way you're brought up has such a lot to do with it. I think here class is changing all the time. A lot of it is racial. A lot of it is where you're brought up as well, from which part of the country you come. Here a lot more people can start off on equal footing.

ABOUT THE PHOTOGRAPH:

Mrs. Ridley: Emily looks a little bit too shy. But the photograph puts us in the right sort of environment anyway.

Mr. Ridley: In the kitchen.

Mrs. Ridley: It's where we spend most of our time.

SOPHIE AND ISADORE FISHMAN

MRS. FISHMAN: Volunteer worker
MR. FISHMAN: Lawyer

Mrs. Fishman: We moved here six years ago, primarily because of the convenience and accessibility to the Loop. My husband's office is located there. We like the area because it's very heterogeneous, and we have the park and the lake right out our window. We used to have a large house and our children had left, so we decided to move closer into the city.

Mr. Fishman: I grew up in a small town in northern Indiana, about twenty-five miles from Chicago, one of the steel mill towns. It was inhabited largely by immigrants from Europe, primarily immigrants from central Europe who came to work in the steel mills and the oil refineries. As a kid I found very little resentment of Jew or Gentile or Pole or whatever it was. We were mostly kids. We didn't know about those things.

My father had come to this country as a boy of about eleven or twelve from a little town near the Minsk marshes. Depending on what year it was, it was either Poland or Russia. He came to the United States and was a tailor by trade. He and my mother met about five years after he arrived and they were married, both at eighteen. She was a poor lady in a sweatshop and he had his own tailor shop. They were on the South Side of Chicago. Well, I was born at Twenty-sixth and State. And I would say they didn't like Chicago particularly. And so they settled in East Chicago, the small town I spoke of in northern Indiana.

Actually in my childhood our family consisted of my mother's father and mother, my mother's sister, three brothers, my father, my sister, and a maid—all living in one house.

Mrs. Fishman: And every Monday his mother ironed thirty-five shirts because there were seven men in the house.

Mr. Fishman: I don't see how they did it. I don't remember too many arguments. But I think the pressures in those

ABOUT THE PHOTOGRAPHS:

Mr. Fishman: Well, frankly, if I were to look at a picture like A, I would say that it looks like a picture of a rather smug, self-satisfied type of person. I don't think there is any character in the photograph. I wouldn't want it saved for posterity.

Mrs. Fishman: I think B much more clearly shows our personalities.

Mr. Fishman: Yes, it is a picture of two rather warm, friendly people who are smiling at a photographer in a rather pleasant environment, and rather happy people, I would say.

Mrs. Fishman: Yes, in B we're holding hands. It shows that we like each other after many years of marriage.

Mr. Fishman: We've probably had as good and interesting a marriage as any I've ever seen. I think she's a fantastic wife and undoubtedly the nicest person I've ever known.

Mrs. Fishman: And my husband is a wonderful husband.

days were astronomic. They were so great that they had no time for waging wars between themselves. But I would think Sophie's story about her parents is far more interesting.

Mrs. Fishman: Well, I was born on the South Side too, Thirty-first and Shields, just about where Sox Park is. My father had come from Germany at age fourteen. He came all alone. He had read the *Leatherstocking Tales* by James Fenimore Cooper, so he came to this country looking for Indians and adventures. He settled in the very southern part of Texas where there were other people from his home town in Germany. He also had a brother who lived in Nashville, Tennessee. So my father walked from the southern part of Texas to Nashville, which took him something like three months. He enlisted in the Tennessee Light Infantry, but he was too skinny. After all that three-month walk, he had gotten very skinny. Then his brother in Nashville moved to Chicago, and my father came too.

My mother had lived in a town on the Rhine. She had two sisters living in Chicago, both married at the time. Chicago was having a great World's Fair in 1893, and she came to it. She was seventeen when she came, and she came alone. Anyway, at a wedding she met my father, and they were married. My father was a baker in the basement of their little cottage where they lived. They worked very very hard their first year and saved a great deal of money. They went back to Europe to visit each other's families. They went back in style—first-class on I forget what ship, all dressed up. And they returned to Chicago, and my father continued to be a baker.

My father was very much a freethinker—an agnostic, if you will. But my mother used to sneak in a few words about, "There probably was a God after all," and we'd better be careful. And we had extremely puritanical attitudes in our household. I mean you had to be honest. Absolutely honest. And you were very very modest. There were no swear words. I remember once I got a whipping for saying, "Darn." And we had to exercise and we had

to report each day at lunch what we had learned that day in school. Almost an army! My parents instilled one wonderful thing: a great curiosity about the world. We didn't have many books in the house, but what we had we read and reread, in German and in English.

In 1958 my husband and I went to Germany to see my mother's home, but we would not go as far into Germany as where my father lived. The house is no longer there anyway. The façade is now in the British Museum as an antique.

Mr. Fishman: This was in 1958, and we still felt the impact of the second war.

Mrs. Fishman: We still do. We weren't happy visiting Germany. We didn't buy as much as a postage stamp on our little sojourn into Mama's home town. It is now totally without Jewish people. And the only ones that are there are in the cemetery, with the stones knocked over.

ABOUT THE CHILDREN:

Mrs. Fishman: I think they have really created their own set of values to a very great extent. The things that we considered important—being neatly dressed, having good table manners, being polite to your elders—ah, I mean, these are very superficial things, but all these things are pretty well gone by the boards.

Of course I did react to my own parents, and I guess I was too permissive. I don't think I ever hit my children. Or very rarely. But I explained to them why things were, which my parents did not.

Mr. Fishman: I think there are many things that we did carry on to our children. I think there was a curiosity of world, as Sophie pointed out, including the curiosity about books. I think that we really gave to the three children the value of right and wrong. I think that two of our children have some connotation of a religious background. Now I'm distinguishing that, you understand, from the concept of being Jewish.

LUCIE AND JUAN PANTOJA
CHILDREN: JOHN, LEE

MRS. PANTOJA: Girl Friday
MR. PANTOJA: Factory foreman

Mr. Pantoja: I've been in the United States since I was seven. For the first three years I lived in Pennsylvania. My father went there for dairy farming. It was like a real bad experience, and, you know, I just remember the hard times. I guess that was probably because of our environmental change. You know, coming from Puerto Rico to Pennsylvania. And experiencing those really, really cold winters. That's one thing that I remember—the snow up to our necks. It was really super bad, a hardship, you know. So my father had to find another means of making money. In 1957, we came to Chicago. He got a job at a dough place, where they made dough for pizzas and things. And he kept that job for fifteen years.

Chicago is a nice city in the summer. I hate Chicago winters. You know, I can't handle them physically. I get super colds. I'm just getting over a cold right now, and it's not even winter yet.

Mrs. Pantoja: I love Chicago, more than Juan does. The winters to me are bad, but I forget them. Just like labor pains. And I should hate them worse because I have an allergy to the cold. I break out in hives and I get welts all over my body from the chill. I've had it since I was in third grade.

We lived in New York until I was fourteen. And I loved it. You know, the neighborhood was predominantly Puerto Rican and Italians and we were all raised on the same block. And everybody knew everybody and we went to the same school. We lived in Harlem. I guess my mother knew how bad New York was and that it wasn't getting any better. And maybe that was part of her wanting to come here. But to us, it was fun.

Mr. Pantoja: You know, I'm out to make myself rich. No, not rich. I'm exaggerating there. But what I'm trying to say is I'm out to work for something. And I work hard. My job is assistant superintendent in a factory. We manufacture synthetic rubber, you know. I do it mostly for the money. I don't like the job because I don't like having to discipline people. You know, it's not my line of work. A lot of times, I have hassles with my own people, the Puerto Ricans, and then they call me a racist. Sometimes, the colored people call me the hatchet man. Because they expect me to let them get away with things, and no way I can do that. I treat everybody as equals there.

I'm also doing part time for a B.A. degree in business. That's because we have a goal that's been in the works for a couple of years. It calls for us moving back to Puerto Rico, and my degree would mean a lot there. There's more opportunity for me there to become financially successful. And also I really appreciate that warm climate over there.

Mrs. Pantoja: I'm a gal Friday. That's not my title, but that's what I do. I started out as receptionist and I also do translating, light bookkeeping, the payroll. It's a variety of jobs and I love it. To begin with, I'm a Gemini and I don't like routine things. I get very bored.

ABOUT THE CHILDREN:

Mr. Pantoja: What was not given to me, I'm going to give to my children. I want to be able to make enough money, you know, to make their life easier so that they can get an education. And I mean profession. Sometimes you have to pay to send them to a good school because just by going to the school in your neighborhood, you know, sometimes the environment might not be right.

When we started high school there was like friction already with the Negroes, and there was a lot of Puerto Ricans and Latinos. And there was a lot of fighting and a lot of gangs. I was in a gang, you know, because I was part of that era.

I think a good possibility is that if my father would have been better off, we probably would have been in a different neighborhood. Right? And probably a better school, you know. And right out of high school, I might have just come straight into college. I might have even got some kind of deferment from the army 'cause at that time, they were giving a lot of those if you went to college. But when I was eighteen I was drafted. And then when I came back we got married. And we had to go to work, both of us.

Mrs. Pantoja: I want my kids first of all to be honest. If they're going to make a living like he says, I want them to have an honest living. I don't want them cheating anybody. Or just being selfish. He wants them to be professionals, you know. O.K. Let them be professionals. But I want them to be honest and happy most of all. Doing what they want to do.

I think we're a together family. We're very close. We know what's happening with our kids, with each other. We also have fun together, I think.

THREE WISHES:
Mrs. Pantoja: There's not many things I want. Peace of mind, which I think I more or less have now. And for my kids to be happy. And to have a lot of time for myself. I'm a little selfish as far as that's concerned. I would like at least six uninterrupted hours for me every day.

Mr. Pantoja: I think basically I would wish health, and then I figure love, along with happiness and money.

ABOUT THE PHOTOGRAPH:
Mrs. Pantoja: That was a Saturday the day the picture was taken. So my mother was here then. Normally, she's here on a Saturday or Sunday to see the kids.

Mr. Pantoja: That's us, you know, naturally.

Mrs. Pantoja: We like dressing up, but not often.

Mr. Pantoja: We only dress up for funerals.

Mrs. Pantoja: And weddings. That's about it.

RICA AND RICH BRUMMETT
CHILD: CLAUDIA

MR. BRUMMETT: Tuckpointing and roofing contractor

Mr. Brummett: My office is only about a mile away. So we picked the neighborhood because it's close to my office. It's close to a lot of things that we enjoy—the lake, the beach, downtown. Basically, we've just moved in here, so we don't know anybody.

Until I was fourteen, I lived in Louisville, Kentucky. I didn't really have too much of a family life. Lived with my grandparents, and I came to Chicago to live with my mother when she got married here. And with that marriage, I inherited two stepbrothers and, I think, a nice teenage life, due to the fact that my stepfather had a business—working on buildings, maintenance on buildings, which the kids were allowed to participate in.

Chicago is a very intimate city for me, the whole city. I feel like I understand it. And it seems small. And in my travels around the States, I really find very few places I would like to live at better than Chicago.

I'm a contractor, and I do roofing and tuckpointing—restore the outside of buildings. It's called exterior building maintenance. I'm self-employed. I like the things that I do in that I'm able to get strokes from. And I don't like the things that are negative and there's no possibility of strokes. (Yeah, *strokes* is approval.)

I feel I'm part of, you know, the mass. The mass to me is the big middle class, and I personally feel I fall in it. Obviously, I'm not the jet-set type, and I certainly don't live an exclusive life in any way. And I think I'm caught up in what I call middle-class problems. Like one problem I think is possibly striving to get out of being middle-class, possibly. But the burden in our society, the burden falls on the middle class, to carry the load. And it's that class of people who really bear the brunt and are what I would call the working people of our particular society. I mean I feel I'm conditioned as middle-class, just as a working bee is conditioned for the job. And I think that there's a certain

amount of enjoyment in performing it, obviously. But I would like the freedom really to escape from the middle class. Not to retire in a traditional sense, but to do more of what I would like to do at any one time.

Question: Do you have any hopes or ambitions for your child?

Mr. Brummett: The only ambition that I would like to lay on her would be that she would be able to know about herself. And to know what she wants for herself and to have the ability to get that for herself so that she can live a whole life the way she wants to live it.

THREE WISHES:
Mr. Brummett: I'd like to take my family to Colombia and I'd like to show off my baby. We've never been there together. And you can always wish for a million bucks because, as someone told me once, "There's nothing wrong with me that money wouldn't cure." I would say the big thing for me would be able to spend more time with my family. And I hope our next baby's a boy. Which will be here in December, by the way.

Mrs. Brummett: We were a big family in Colombia, South America. Seven children. And I lived with my parents until I was seventeen. Then I lived with my uncle until I came to the States. I was about twenty-one, twenty-two years old. I came here for a vacation. Came to Miami. And kind of liked it. It was different. So I decided to come here and visit Chicago. I knew my uncle here. But I started studying and found a job. Then I met my husband.

ABOUT THE PHOTOGRAPH:
Mr. Brummett: I think my wife looks much older there, and she's dressed differently. I guess I don't often see her that way. With the advent of pants, I never see her in a dress. And ah, her hair. She's got her hair back and I don't picture my wife with her hair back. I picture my wife with long black hair. Loose, down, right. This makes her look a little more sophisticated. And me. Probably from the expression on my face, it projects a little bit more playfulness than I think I usually look.

CAROL DEWEY
CHILD: LISA

MS. DEWEY: Secretary

I grew up in Harvard, Illinois, a very small town about seventy-five miles from here. I lived there until I was eighteen, with my parents. I wouldn't live there again, but I think it's a great place for a kid to grow up. A lot more freedom, less worry about the kids, no traffic. But it makes no sense to me how someone can live their whole life in that town. A surprising number of people do. I'm not a friendly person, and it bothers me to have every person in the town know you.

The government came recruiting to the high school while I was there. So I filled out the applications and things and was accepted and I moved to Washington. I had the job before I went—secretarial work—and they paid for my transportation and they paid to ship all of my clothes and things. I loved Washington. I stayed for three years. But I was bored. Also Lisa became two and a half and it was too expensive to fly home to see my parents. I have wished a million times I hadn't left.

Yes, I have always been on my own. People have always told me that it's such an admirable thing to do and I keep thinking, "Oh wow, I'm admirable. That's really nice." But I can't really see it myself. In fact, a girl called me a few days ago. She is thinking of separating from her husband and she says she just doesn't see how it can possibly be done. How can she live on her own and support her son? And she said she has been thinking of me constantly. You know, it has been real simple. I guess I just take it for granted after all this time. Everything came very easily. I was kind of surprised myself. I really haven't had any big problems at all since I've been on my own. I think I was ready for it. I was anxious to leave Harvard. Counting the days.

THREE WISHES:

I would wish for more money. I would like to not have to work full-time. Besides being unfriendly, I'm also lazy. I would like the freedom to try other things besides secretarial work. I just kind of fell into it because I wasn't trained for anything else and I don't have any education beyond high school. I've tried to think of different areas that I might be interested in, but I just haven't come up with anything. Right now I need the security of the job. So I can't quit and go looking for something else. For now, I'm pretty much stuck where I am. My third wish? For Lisa's happiness. It doesn't really matter if she's rich or if she's poor or what kind of work she's doing, whether she's married or has children, as long as she's happy.

I'm basically content with the way my life is now. Content is just being, you know, happy enough with the way things are at the moment. I don't see how my life will change drastically. If I were to get married I think that would be a big change. But I'm not planning on it. I probably will stay single.

Question: How do you feel about being in a book?

My immediate reaction would be that it would be nice to have all these people looking at my picture and reading about me. I have a curiosity about other people. Like I read Studs Terkel. I wish that he had pictures in his book, because I think it means more if you can see the people, too. But my next reaction would be wondering if anything I have said would hurt anyone's feelings or making someone angry, somebody I know. I don't have a big sense of privacy. Some people are really sensitive about how much rent they pay or how much a thing costs them. I don't mind things like that or personal-type questions.

ABOUT THE PHOTOGRAPH:

I think we both look, especially my daughter, a little strained and a little tense, with kind of a fakey smile. But then she always turns out that way in pictures. I do think the photograph reflects me. The lamps and other objects in the room are mine. The photographs and pictures on the wall belong to my roommate. And I'm glad the cat is in the picture.

TERESA OSTIMER
MARGARET PETERSON
(her mother)

CHILD: BRIDGET

MRS. OSTIMER: Clerk
MRS. PETERSON: Volunteer worker

Mrs. Peterson: We have foreign origin, you know, my mother was from Ireland and, of course, on my father's side they're four generations American, so I consider myself a typical American family.

Mrs. Ostimer: Oh, I don't know whether we're that typical. You know, like myself, divorced woman going back home with her parents. A lot of people say it's hard to go back home. But we're making it. I've been back three years, ever since my husband walked out.

Mrs. Peterson: "Grandma Pete" they call me. I'm grandma for everybody. And everyone around here, all nationalities, it doesn't make any difference, they're all my grandchildren. Sometimes a black girl will run up to me on the street and kiss me. "Hi, Grandma." And people sometimes will stare. But it doesn't bother me because I love everybody. They all come with their problems, the big and the little. And talk to me. Anybody that's in trouble with the welfare and stuff. 'Cause everybody has to have somebody, a sounding block in other words, to get it out of their system.

Mrs. Ostimer: She reads tea leaves too.

Mrs. Peterson: I've had a happy' life. I've got six living children, thank God, and they all give me happiness. And thirty grandchildren and five great-grandchildren. Some people say, "Oh children, you know, you're overpopulating the world." Well, I don't know. With the rate that people are dying, I don't see how we're overpopulating.

Mrs. Ostimer: Now what we call the neighborhood is just basically the projects.

Mrs. Peterson: It's just like a little town, I would say. I've been here for twenty-four years.

Mrs. Ostimer: It's starting to kind of split up. Before, it was like the people were here to make it go. Now I don't know. The neighbors are fighting with neighbors. It's more or less the new people coming in. I never thought I would be scared, and this is starting to scare me. Just like the other day. A really calm and relaxed woman just took a meat cleaver. Got into an argument with another lady and the lady is in critical condition.

Mrs. Peterson: Your dope. It's dope that is really the problem.

Mrs. Ostimer: And what gets you is the police know exactly where it's at and they do nothing about it. They know exactly where the guns are, too. But they just don't care.

Mrs. Peterson: Now everybody bawls me out for leaving my doors open. Anybody knocks, I say, "Come in." I say, "I've never been afraid in all these years. I'm not going to start altering my ways and lock my doors." Because there's a Supreme Being watching over me, and I know he's not going to let any harm come to me unless it's supposed to happen.

ABOUT THE PHOTOGRAPH:

Mrs. Ostimer: Well, it looks like we're close. You know, three generations right there.

Mrs. Peterson: It's a homey picture.

Mrs. Ostimer: Well, we got prepared for the picture, but it wasn't like we overdid it. Like, you know, when you go to a photographer's studio. It's just like us. Right here.

Mrs. Peterson: I didn't expect to get in the picture at all. Remember? I was sitting in the kitchen and you asked me to come in for the last picture.

BETTY AND TOM HANNIGAN
CHILDREN: SHAUN, KENNY

MRS. HANNIGAN: Editor for insurance company
MR. HANNIGAN: Assistant manager, order department

Mrs. Hannigan: I was born in Lorraine, Ohio, a real small town. And my parents were poor. But we did not know it; we were quite content. My father was a baker, like my grandparents were. After I got out of high school, because there were no jobs in Lorraine, I came here. And I chose Chicago because my sister lived here and I figured at least I'd know one person.

I came to Chicago about 1965. And I like it here. I love it here, in fact. If you want to be friendly, there are people to be friendly. If you don't want your neighbor to know you blew your nose, he isn't going to. You can be what you want to be in the city, and there isn't going to be any hassle over it.

I don't want to be a suburbanite. I know this may be just prejudice because I'm living in the city, but I know an awful lot of suburban people. And you can have them. You can usually tell who they are when they're in a crowd. There's just something about them.

I suppose in one way it would be better for the kids to be out in the country. But there are still a lot of city experiences, you know, that help them to get a better perspective on life. When we were in school, our friends were Johnny and Susie and Mary, and we learned a certain number of things from them, most of which you already knew from your own family because they were exact duplicates of your family. My son goes to school with Manuel and Sukiookiyaha and all those crazy things and he learns so much from them. He knows more at his age than I knew at twenty-five, and I think it's fantastic.

My son says he doesn't want to live in a city. And I think this is ground into him at school because he comes home with these fancy words about, "Oh, it's too polluted around here," and all of that jazz.

The one thing that I think we miss now, the thing that I had when I was a kid, is having the aunts and uncles and the grandparents around them. That's what my children miss, and they don't even know they're missing it. But my grandparents are dead and my mother is dead and all my brothers and sisters are scattered all over the United States. So it's very seldom that we get to see each other.

I'm an editor for a large organization, and I love my work. Tommy once asked me, "If we had a million dollars tomorrow, would you work?" My answer is "Yes." I couldn't stand to be home all day, every day.

Mr. Hannigan: I lived in Chicago all my life except the time I spent in the service. I grew up on the South Side of Chicago, a couple different neighborhoods. And these neighborhoods kind of turned, so to speak, and my parents felt they had to move further out. My dad always had to work two jobs but there was always food on the table and clothes on our backs and enough for a few extra things. He worked full-time as a carpenter on the railroad and then he worked on weekends as a cabdriver. Now he's only working the one job and, you know, honestly he's gotten to the point where he's learned how to relax a little bit and enjoy life. It took him a long time.

I'm an assistant manager of the order department for a firm. There are twelve people in the department, and I have to schedule their vacations and keep track of the attendance, turn in the time sheets. The biggest part of my job is all the quotations that go out. I process all of them. Most of the time I have no complaints about the job at all. I like it.

I never went to college. Now, having two kids and seeing the way prices are going up and seeing the way my salary is slowly going up, I wish I had gone to college.

ABOUT THE PHOTOGRAPH:

Mrs. Hannigan: Well, I hate to say this, because the word has a lot of connotations that I don't care for, but to me it looks like the typical average American family with two kids. What do I mean by average? Well, average income, two children, nothing spectacular about the surroundings, pleasant.

MARY AND VINCENT BARRERA
CHILDREN: JOSE, MARIO, ISABEL, CHRISTINA SANTIAGO
GRANDCHILD: NICOLE
AUNT: MARIA SEGOVIA

MRS. BARRERA: Spot welder
MR. BARRERA: Machinist

Mr. Barrera: I have been in Chicago for about thirty-eight years. During the forties, I was in Mexico, and I decided to better myself by coming over here. I told my mother there was a big request for manpower in the United States and that I wanted to come over. I was sixteen years of age. At that time she didn't want me to come because the war was going on and she thought for sure I was going to be drafted and sent out to the front lines. But it didn't happen that way. Before the age of eighteen the war was over. However, when I was twenty-six there was the Korean situation and I was in the service at that time. But that's a different story.

At that time my mother also told me I was an American. You see, my parents had left Mexico around the time of the revolution. My mother was maybe twelve, fifteen years of age. She and my father met in Tennessee in the 1920s—something like that. And afterwards they moved north to Pennsylvania, where I was born. That's why I have American nationality.

Mrs. Barrera: I was born in Phoenix, Arizona, but I came from Central America, from San Salvador. I first came to New York and I stayed about one year. And then I came to Chicago. I met my husband over here and three months later we were married. For me Chicago is better than any other place. I like it.

Mr. Barrera: I accept Chicago. It is a place that I live in. I make a living here. I have been able to support a family. We have a home. And no place else have I accomplished this. In that sense I do like Chicago, but this is not necessarily loving it.

Mario: Last year I went to Mexico. I stayed with my relatives over there. It was beautiful. I loved it for a visit, but I would hate to live there because I couldn't stand to see all those poor people, day after day. You know, the people on the corners with their hands out. I'm proud of what I am, my ancestors. It makes me feel good. Like if I were to leave Chicago for about twenty, twenty-five years and come back, it wouldn't be that same kind of feeling I have about Mexico.

Mr. Barrera: I'm a machinist, toolmaker. I just learned that before I went to the army. And I have been lucky. In my job they consider me the assistant foreman. The money is not too bad. Moneywise the improvement of the family has been better than if I would have stayed in Mexico. As far as the kids are concerned, I do wish they will benefit from everything we are doing for them. This is the most we can give them, the best we can afford to give them. This is one of the reasons we have chosen to stay here—to give them an advantage to better themselves. The future? No better, no worse. I would be happy to just have the same things I have now.

ABOUT THE PHOTOGRAPH:

Mr. Barrera: The woman in the middle of the photograph is my aunt. She was lost for fifty-some years. Around 1915 she ran away from home in Mexico because of the revolution. And fifty years later she looked for my mother who is her sister. She was able through relatives in northern Mexico to find my mother. We are happy and enjoy seeing her. This is the second time she was at our house.

Question: Is the photograph at all misleading?

Mr. Berrera: "Misleading" would be that the subconscious part of the individual, his inner feelings, would be different than what the picture shows. No picture can take that.

JOANNE SANDOVAL
CHILDREN: JENNIFER, JESSE

MS. SANDOVAL: Part-time student

We moved to this neighborhood because I take care of the building and get free rent and because it is close to my sister-in-law's. Before I was living with my mother on the Southwest Side of Chicago. I really feel that this is a great neighborhood in all ways. Everybody's doing their own thing. Nobody's getting stepped on, you know. You could be homosexuals living next to call girls living next to perfectly straight people and nobody minds. I know there are a lot of robberies in this neighborhood, but I've never known anybody that's been robbed. And it's very friendly. Just about everybody you pass on the street says, "Hi."

My parents' idea of security is having your own home and a car or two and maybe a color TV set. They think you can't be secure if you live in an apartment. Really, I don't feel that way. I just like to be myself. I guess their possessions are so important to them because they came from immigrants. They had nothing. My father's parents came from Czechoslovakia and they both came here with absolutely nothing and scrimped and saved. And my mother's parents were very poor, too. They had lots of kids and poor medical care and lived in a cramped city apartment, and my grandfather finally got enough money to build a house in the country.

Security to me is just knowing that I'm going to have the money to pay the bills when they come up, just having a steady income, but not necessarily having a lot of money. I have to depend on child-support payments from my former husband and I can't always be sure of getting them. So when there's no money coming from there, that means I have to go out and earn money sort of on the spur of the moment. I can't have jobs all the time because I'm going to college part-time. But I do have to work occasionally just to make ends meet. I really want to be self-sufficient and not have to rely on child support.

My kids have to be very secure before they'll let a man come in and have some of my attention. They have to really feel loved. So it's a matter of always showing them that I love them first. And a lot of men aren't grown up enough to wait for their turn.

I've never really had a chance to live a single life. You know, I'd still kind of like to know what that's like. I was eighteen when I got married. I graduated from high school when I was seventeen, and I worked for a year and then I got married to a boy I had met in my senior year. So instead of moving out of my mother's house and living on my own, I moved in with a man.

ABOUT THE PHOTOGRAPH:

Yes, I'd say it's a fair description. Jennifer always acts very shy and she looks kind of shy in that picture, and Jesse is sitting way forward with a big grin on his face and he's very aggressive and outgoing. And I'm just the mother, and I just sort of sit there and let it all happen.

Question: Did you prepare for the photograph?

I put on makeup, which I had almost never done up until that point. I had thought it wasn't in keeping with my idea of what a mother should be. But at group therapy my therapist said I'm shying away from people and that I'm using this drab look so people won't notice me. I'm finding that it works exactly the way the therapist said; if I wear makeup I sort of stand out and meet people, and if I don't I sort of fade out.

SHARON AND MARK KLARICH

CHILDREN: BRANDON, JUSTIN, SUZANNE, LYNNE, LILA, LAURA, LISETTE

MR. KLARICH: Actor/director working as an auditor

Mr. Klarich: Around four years ago we went away to Europe, to Rome, and it was supposed to be forever. It was wonderful except for the money. So after a year, we decided to come back to Chicago, where we have connections to make some money. Coming back has given us the capability of pulling enough things together so that when we make our next jump it won't be quite so shoestring.

Chicago is no place for human beings. I mean, in order to live here you have to go through daily duress that's really inhuman. It's not fair to the human psyche.

Mrs. Klarich: There's nothing conducive to a feeling of goodness. My husband is white and I'm not. Every move is a move into a different racist environment. When we were in Europe we dealt with that, but there was no fear of bodily harm. And that's very important. Because here there is the constant possibility of physical harm. The other thing that is so unpleasant here is that one must automatically assume that any strange person is going to harm you. Everyone has to start at zero and build their way up. And there's something inside me that doesn't want to do that.

Mr. Klarich: Americans are so inherently violent anyway. It's the fighting every day not to be part of it.

Mrs. Klarich: It's the taking karate and the buying of guns and the traps that people set for each other.

Mr. Klarich: And having to prepare yourself for the eventu-

ABOUT THE PHOTOGRAPHS:

Mr. Klarich: The outdoors shot has got more depth and more movement to it, more composition. And we both prefer it. It's not as strict and formal as the inside picture is.

Mrs. Klarich: And we're outside people. I think that's where we'd rather be. We like the space, the freedom, the movement, and that outdoors picture says that. You know, we're spread out in that picture, and there is something very sprawling about us. An ideal picture of us would probably be dressed the same way but in front of a cabin or a house surrounded by forest and BLM [Bureau of Land Management] land.

Mr. Klarich: We've already pretty well decided that you'll probably use the indoors picture. It fits within your motif, like the pictures we've seen of the other two families.

Mrs. Klarich: I suppose for a family portrait the outdoors picture is so unorthodox.

ality, and it is an eventuality, of someone coming through your front door. And you have to live with the possibility that if you stop to pick up somebody who's hitchhiking, he might kill you.

Mrs. Klarich: It's not the greater fear because we're a mixed couple, but it's a greater isolation. We're almost isolationists. We've selected our environment to the point that racism is not so much of an issue. We keep it down to a minimum.

People in the inner city where I grew up are stuck, for the most part. Even if you make enough money to get out, you're stuck because you don't know where to go. But you see, the confinement for a mixed couple is even greater because you can't go and live in my old neighborhood. And you certainly can't go and live in Cicero and many other places.

Mr. Klarich: But really, there's a lot of freedom in knowing that you can't depend on anybody but yourself. All I have is Sharon and some very selected close friends that I can depend on to a certain extent.

Our plan is to go to the country. Probably to Colorado. And we hope to go by the end of the summer. A year ago we went on vacation and ended up in Colorado. It was nice, and it was one of the few places where we've been that people didn't stare at us or say anything when we got out of the car. And they were friendly to us. And we loved the mountains.

Mrs. Klarich: Yes, I want to get out of here. I never lived in a house, never in my life. The closest I came to anything that was really mine was when we lived in a tent.

Mr. Klarich: Our master plan is to have a house we can always come back to. And we want to raise our own food.

Right now I'm working as an auditor for the state because you can't make any money in the theater, not in Chicago anyway, and not in the beginning levels anywhere. Our hope is when we do leave these parts and go to the country, we'll either start or become very active in the local community theater. I'm interested in ritual theater and developing new forms of expression.

ABOUT THE CHILDREN:
Mrs. Klarich: I like those little people, our children. They're my kind of people. They're all very helpful, although sometimes I go crazy. Mark has taught me to relax, and the only thing about it is that it kind of backfired, because instead of showing me how to relax, he gave me his relaxation and now we are all in the process of calming him down.

Mr. Klarich: By being products of a mixed marriage, our children are constantly being faced with the horrors of racism in a way that we're not. What is required of them in many cases is a kind of adult behavior. And yet we demand that they sort out the different forms of racism. I'm more interested in their being able to ferret out the truth than add nine and nine.

THREE WISHES:
Mr. Klarich: I would wish for an end to all war. And successful colonization of other planets. And I would wish that one of my children would be able to go to one of those planets.

Mrs. Klarich: I would wish for a cure for cancer and a guarantee that everything I wrote would be published and make some money. I don't have to sell *Jaws* or *Fear of Flying* all over again. But I want to make just enough money by writing so that Mark would never have to go to work for anyone else again. And, probably I would wish that I could save my children, or my children could save themselves, from the army and the muggers and the rapists and the Charlie Mansons. And I would like to have just five dollars a day to blow out there on the western slopes of the Rockies, so that when I want to go in and take everybody to see *Journey to Witch Mountain*, or whatever the latest Disney flick is, or if we pass an amusement park, we can take everybody for a round on the Ferris wheel. Or maybe it means Pilsner instead of Schlitz, you know, or maybe it means I don't have to cook today. Five dollars just to blow, money that was not meant to pay for a shot or another case of soybean milk.

BARBARA AND JERRY KAISER
CHILDREN: PETER, PAUL

MRS. KAISER: Nurse
MR. KAISER: Florist

Mrs. Kaiser: I think basically what people try to do is just raise their children to be healthy—mentally and physically as well. You try to raise children so that they know what's going on around them . . . to be able to make decisions on their own as they get older.

Mr. Kaiser: We've raised our children somewhat as a modification of a pacifist because we don't believe in guns. And we don't allow our children to have guns.

Mrs. Kaiser: And they go to a school—St. Vincent's—where this is enforced, too.

Mr. Kaiser: At St. Vincent's, they do not allow children to have guns, and children are not allowed to pretend that they have a gun. Like bang, bang, bang type of thing. And it's explained to them why. And we respect that a great deal about St. Vincent's.

Mrs. Kaiser: When they get older, if they want to go into the service or if they want to have guns of their own—that has to be their own choice when they get older.

Mr. Kaiser: Besides the guns, we participate in the United Farm Workers boycott on lettuce and grapes. And they have been, ever since Paul has been two and a half, you know, in boycott strikes and in picket lines and all sorts of things. And he knows exactly why he doesn't eat lettuce. And if we go out to someone's house and he says, you know, "Is this a union lettuce?" or, "Is this a lettuce that I can eat?" And if someone says, "No, it's not," then he'll say, "Then why are you eating it?" Paul is seven. He also does that with people who smoke. 'Cause we don't smoke and we don't believe that it's healthy for people to smoke. And he'll say, "You're going to get cancer if you smoke."

Mrs. Kaiser: But sometimes you can enforce it too much and you really make it a hangup to some kids.

Mr. Kaiser: Except that our boys are able to explain why they are doing things.

Mrs. Kaiser: Of course, our ideals are not always the greatest in the world, too. I mean, we're not perfect. And, you know, I think you just try to enforce things, but they have minds of their own and they'll have to make their choices and their decisions. Just like we don't have basically the same ideals as our parents do.

You ask about the families we came from. My family was a fairly passive family. And they were fairly strict. They're a German family, you know, very clean and meticulous. If you did something wrong, my mother was the typical person who always thought it would reflect on her. My father was an accountant. And so he was a very precise type of person. He had a photographic memory. He impressed upon us when we were kids never to answer a question or never to say anything unless it's perfect and it's the exact thing to say. Not a lot of freedom to say what you really wanted to. But there was a lot of loving in the family.

I grew up on the South Side of Chicago, not too far away from where my parents grew up. And where I went to high school was just down the street from where they went to high school. So basically, you know, we didn't stray too far from Sixty-third and Kedzie, Fifty-fifth and Kedzie. My parents have lived in the same house for like forty years.

Mr. Kaiser: We grew up in a somewhat similar neighborhood as Barbara did. On the South Side of Chicago. My parents had five children, and we were all born in the early forties and mid-forties. My father was not involved in the war. He was a packinghouse worker. A meatpacker. And we had a very difficult sort of thing because they were on strike a great deal of the time. He was always at a union meeting. And it was very difficult for my mother to raise five children. In about 1956 we moved to a suburb, to sort of a country suburb, Midlothian. Now it is all built up. And they still live there.

Mrs. Kaiser: I work full-time and that's because things are so expensive. And so that we live off my salary now. What

Jerry makes in the store we put back into the store, so there's some revenue in the store. I'm a nurse and I enjoy my work. It's fulfilling my self-image. I enjoy working in the OB Department. What I thoroughly enjoy about my job is when a baby is born. I just stare. I think it is the most fantastic thing in the world. When a baby is born lots of lives go ahead of you and you wonder where it all came from. You really do.

Mr. Kaiser: I pretty much enjoy my work because I do what I want and I please the people that I want. I'm choosy about who I really want to have as a customer. I don't like to be mistreated. If people are rude, I don't want their business, and I make it very clear to them that I don't want them to come in and buy things from me. And most people find out very soon that if they let me do what I think is right for them, they get a much better arrangement than if they tell me what to do. I'm my own boss. I set my own hours. I set my own prices. I think there's a lot more to being a florist than most people think there is. I'm not a big booster about myself, but I feel that I'm creating a feeling or a particular form of art for individuals. And it also involves a lot of philosophy with it. We think about what the person would like or what the whole aspect of the wedding is going to look like. That's the big difference between our shop and most other people. They just don't have standards—they sell flowers and they don't care if it's the wrong color rose or the wrong kind of flower.

ABOUT THE PHOTOGRAPH:

Mr. Kaiser: Yes, we felt it was a fair description of us. That's why we like it.

Mrs. Kaiser: Well, Paul is holding a flower and he's pushing it forward. You know, he's always very excited about flowers. Peter looks like a little clown. And that's what he does most frequently—clown. And Jerry is very proud of his hat.

Mr. Kaiser: Just that I was bound and determined to wear a hat. . . . And there is sweet, demure Barbara. . . . It just emphasizes the fact that we really lived in that flower shop and never really lived upstairs in the apartment above the shop.

JEAN HOLMAN AND LARRY FREEMAN

MS. HOLMAN: Public relations worker, government agency
MR. FREEMAN: Communications consultant, phone company

Ms. Holman: Well, I'm transplanted from Springfield, Illinois. Springfield was the kind of place where people didn't lock doors and there were gardens in the back yards and kids bicycling in the street. It really was idyllic. And then all that was interrupted when I moved here when I was ten.

My mother had been widowed at twenty-five. My father's death was service-related. So when he died she came from southern California—where I was born, by the way—to Springfield, where her mother lived. She stayed for a while and tried to like it, but she just couldn't hack it. It was too quiet. So she moved to Chicago. It was a good move for her.

When I came to Chicago I just went through a whole lot of shock, because in Springfield I had gone to an integrated school—actually there were only six blacks in my class—and then I came here and I went to an all-black school because it was a segregated neighborhood. And beside that I had to go from like twenty-five kids in a classroom to forty. After my first year here the whole school went on double shifts. I hated Chicago for a long time. I used to go back to Springfield every summer, and I loved it.

Mr. Freeman: I'm from New Orleans originally, and that's where my family is now. My father worked for the Post Office and he still does. I went to the same schools and the same church and everything that my parents did. But I quickly became very bored with it. I just wanted something different. And I left to go to high school, boarding school, in New York. I loved it, you know. I really did. It was the first time I'd ever been out of the South.

Ms. Holman: We've come to like living in a highrise. I remember one time a friend of mine and I were talking about an apartment complex called Lake Meadows, and she said, "Oh, that project." I remember that I was very

insulted and I said, "That's not a project. That's a highrise." At the time I couldn't think of the difference. But the difference is when people want to live in a certain place and can live comfortably, you can stack people up as tall as you want. But when they don't want to live there and it's overcrowded, that's a whole different thing.

Question: Can you put yourselves in a class?

Mr. Freeman: I went to college in the late sixties. I suppose that was the period when I personally flourished to a very great degree. And I sort of hold that period very dear to my heart. And so you can say that I am in a class now of young people—you know, working, career people.

Ms. Holman: You know, I think class is a state of mind more than a state of money. I mean, if you are doing what you want to, or trying to, and have positive feelings about yourself, then you're a first-class or upper-class person.

Mr. Freeman: My family was middle-class because of their attitudes.

Ms. Holman: Church on Sunday, two cars . . .

Mr. Freeman: Grow up and get married and have children . . .

Ms. Holman: Care what the neighbors think . . . I can say wholeheartedly we don't endorse any of those things.

THREE WISHES:
Ms. Holman: Our immediate dreams are to move to France. He's going to teach English as a foreign language and I want to go to school and we both want to write. And we'd like not to starve to death in the process.

Mr. Freeman: We're working on the dream and we're pretty confident that it's going to work out.

ABOUT THE PHOTOGRAPH:
Ms. Holman: The photograph seems very formal, and we're very informal.

Mr. Freeman: I think there's a pretty obvious glow, and it sort of indicates the fact that we're pretty much happy with the type of lives we have now, in our home life, and everything.

VERONICA AND MIGUEL DAKESSIAN
CHILDREN: VICTOR, ROBERTO

MRS. DAKESSIAN: Teacher, keypunch operator
MR. DAKESSIAN: Shoemaker

Mrs. Dakessian: I am Armenian. My grandmother and all the family escaped from the Turkish massacre in 1915. My grandmother went to the south coast of the Mediterranean. Later, in 1929, she went to Jerusalem. I was born in Jerusalem, in the British government. My father was a barber in the Old City. I was there until 1951. Then I went to Cyprus to study high school. After I received my diploma, I went back to Jerusalem with my grandmother until my papers came. Then I went to Argentina. That was 1957.

My mother and my sister were in Argentina, so I went there. I started to work as a teacher in the Armenian school. I taught big children, sixth, seventh grades. I taught Armenian, grammar, history, religion. I also was teaching Armenian folklore. After two years I got married to Miguel.

Mr. Dakessian: My origins are also Armenian. I was born in Kalymnos, an island in Greece, in 1931. Before the Turkish massacre, in 1913 or 1914, my grandfather went to the island. He was in a safe place. My father was only five or six years old when they escaped to the island. My father lived on the island most of his life. He met and married my mother there. He had a grocery, and they made coffee and candies. When I was born the Italians were on the island. Now in the Second World·War they gave it to the Greeks.

I went to Argentina with a Greek passport in 1949. I lived almost twenty-two years in Argentina. After one year I brought my sisters and brothers and father from Greece. I liked Argentina because it was far from all the wars. I suffered a lot from all the wars.

I've had many jobs. Of all the jobs I liked furmaking best, because it was fine. It was delicate. I had a small fur coat factory in Argentina, with employees and everything.

I came to the United States with a contract for making furs in New York. But it fell through after I got there, because one of the owners of the factory died. I didn't have anywhere to go. Then I remembered I had a friend in Chicago. I came to visit him and liked it better here than in New York. And I thought of doing this job of shoemaker. I didn't want to go to the factories. I wanted to do something on my own. I sometimes make fur coats here— synthetic furs, because the natural is very expensive.

I wanted to bring my children here because there was more opportunity for the future. More opportunity in getting jobs, to go to college. I have been here five years, so this year I will become a citizen.

THREE WISHES:
I want my children to be better than I am, to study more than I did, to be better. We didn't have the opportunity during the war to do that. Second wish: that God helps me to buy my own house. And third wish: maybe a different job.

Mrs. Dakessian: Chicago at first was strange. It was so cold in December and January. And as a rule, the people are so busy, they're working so hard, you have no time to make some visits.

I don't want to move any more because it's too hard. New people, new relationships, new language if you go to a different country. But if I go to another place, I will like this life in Chicago. Always it's the same. You remember your sweet past life. When I went to Argentina I cried too much. I was remembering my friends, my high school in Cyprus. But now after I came here, I'm always longing for Argentina.

ABOUT THE PHOTOGRAPH:
Mrs. Dakessian: We feel honored by the picture.

MILDRED AND ALBERT GROTH

MR. GROTH: Retired truck mechanic

Mrs. Groth: We've been in this neighborhood all our lives. For the most part the neighborhood used to be German, with a few Italian, few Polish, few Irish. Today, it's still mixed.

Mr. Groth: As far as I know, my grandparents came from the border of Germany and Poland.

Mrs. Groth: And mine came from Germany. My grandmother spoke German to us. And she dressed like an old German lady, with the long dress and a little white apron on the front, you know. My mother talked to her in English and my grandmother would answer her in German.

Mr. Groth: About living in the city, I like it. And when you look at the way people move to the suburbs. If I had to go through stuff like that, forget it.

Mrs. Groth: We're still here. I think that says something. You know, in the city you don't have to depend on a car if you don't want to. And my church is quite important to me, and that's close by. I was active in the Y for a long, long time. And that's a mile away. And shopping is close by. So it's convenient.

Mr. Groth: And they say that the neighborhood is changing today. To me it's still the same as it was twenty-five, thirty years ago.

Mrs. Groth: My oldest sister was living in a suburb and she came to visit. And she walked down my street with me and I knew everyone and talked to everyone as I went down. And she said, "Don't ever move." She said, "You don't know what a feeling it is to walk down the street and not know a soul."

Mr. Groth: I was a truck mechanic. It was the best years of my life. Before that I did a lot of different jobs. The first job I had, I worked in a gold-pounding place where they take and make gold leaf. And I went on a milk wagon and I was delivering flowers for a florist. But doing truck repair work, well, that's what I done the biggest part of my life. And it was hard work, but I enjoyed it.

Mrs. Groth: And Al was in charge of the garage. He was fleet superintendent. But if you ask him he would just say he's a truck mechanic.

Mr. Groth: I like being retired. More- relaxed, no tension. Retiring was the easiest thing in the world for me to do 'cause I just left my tools down at work and gave them to my son. Yes, he's a truck mechanic, too.

Mrs. Groth: Besides our son who's a truck mechanic, we also have a son who's a plant manager who lives in Iowa. And we have a daughter who is a graduate nurse, who lives in Michigan.

Question: How do you feel about being in a book?

Mrs. Groth: It struck me as kind of funny, because one of my friends always tells me she is going to write a book about me. There's always something happening in my life and she'll say, "Oh, there's another page in your book." And I sort of took it as fate when you called.

ABOUT THE PHOTOGRAPH:

Mrs. Groth: I think you see our home, our lifestyle, more in the one you've chosen. I love my pictures that show in the background.

Mr. Groth: Getting me to pose for a picture is the hardest thing in the world to get me to do. Because I don't do it. I'm just natural, that's all. What I am, I am, and they take me for what I am, and if they don't I can't help it.

Mrs. Groth: I think he's trying to say he's not going to put on a front to take a picture.

Mr. Groth: Not for anybody.

Mrs. Groth: He won't pretend to be something that he's not.

MARLYS AND JULIAN STYNE

MRS. STYNE: College English teacher
MR. STYNE: Federal marshal

Mr. Styne: My father ran away from home when he was fourteen and joined the circus. He was a flyer and a clown. And then he came from Boston to Chicago and met my mother. She was going to college to be a teacher, and they got married and he gave up the circus. For a while he was a steeplejack. And then he settled down and worked for a newspaper distributor. He drove a newspaper truck until he retired. I grew up in Chicago.

Mrs. Styne: I was born on a farm in Whitewater, Wisconsin. I never liked the farm. It was a medium-sized farm and not very successful. My father's parents had been quite wealthy and raised cattle for show and so on. But they lost everything during the Depression. All the time I was on the farm I was reading about other places that I wanted to go to. England was one of them, and Chicago was another. At seventeen I went away to college and I never really lived there after that.

Mr. Styne: I'm a deputy United States marshal. I find law enforcement very fascinating and fulfilling. Unfortunately it does get boring sometimes, but usually by the time it does, there's always something else to do. Our bureau enforces federal court orders. We look for people who haven't come in on bonds, we see to the security of federal courtrooms, federal judges, congressional committees, and we transport federal prisoners.

Preceding all of the law enforcement work I owned the Old Town Pub. It was an English-type pub that catered to neighborhood people. A large commercial operation. I ran it for seven years. That was a really wild growth period in this neighborhood, when people were renovating buildings and many younger people were moving in.

Mrs. Styne: We've had the house for about five or six years, and before that we both lived in the suburbs.

Mr. Styne: Marlys and I were married before and lived in different suburbs.

Mrs. Styne: We both broke up our marriages at different times and sort of started again.

Mr. Styne: That was about the time that I gave up the saloon and went into what you would call a straight job. It probably saved my health. I'll tell you that in the saloon business you've got to listen to all the stories and be sympathetic and tell people what they want to hear. At a certain point I was not tolerant any longer. I had to quit.

THREE WISHES:

Mrs. Styne: I don't think I could think of three things I want, except more of the good life we've had.

Mr. Styne: I think we're at the point in life now where we have the rewards of our work. We don't have the things to worry about that young families have.

Mrs. Styne: We feel now that we can do pretty much what we want to, within reason.

ABOUT THE PHOTOGRAPHS:

Mrs. Styne: I think we look comfortable, happy, both trying to smile.

Mr. Styne: Perhaps we are dressed one notch up from working around the house and three notches down from going to work.

ANN ESPINOSA
CHILDREN: NAOMA, GIANNA, CHRISTOPHER, CARI, LUIS

MRS. ESPINOSA: Admitting clerk in hospital; part-time college student

We kind of take each minute or each hour as it comes, play everything by ear. If it's a nice day, if nothing is really pressing, well, we might leave the laundry go one night. We might stop at McDonald's and pick up some hamburgers and go to Lincoln Park instead. I mean, the laundry will be there tomorrow, but tomorrow might not be such a nice day. Whenever I've tried to stick to a really rigid schedule, everybody usually gets very nervous and uptight and we end up screaming at each other a lot.

This is my old neighborhood. I grew up here. When I was six we moved to a suburb, but we moved back to the city when I was twelve. Basically I think the neighborhood is still pretty similar. I probably tend to restrict my children more than I was restricted just because there is also the seamy side of the city. I would never send them down to the neighborhood movie theater alone. It could be *Bambi*, but I wouldn't let them go by themselves because there are situations where they can be taken advantage of.

Oh, I wouldn't move to the suburbs. I don't think I could be confined to a house with a certain little plot of grass because it was the thing to do. There are definitely more rules in the suburbs, and, you know, I make my own rules. Everybody has this big idea: "You've got kids, you've got to move to the suburbs." And I kind of resent it because I think the city is a fabulous place for kids.

I feel more secure in the city. The man next door cuts my front lawn for me. Nobody's ever asked him to. He does it all the time. And I don't think you could find that in the suburbs.

My own background? My mother's parents came from Sweden and Denmark; my father's parents came from Wales and Germany. And they all settled in Minnesota and Iowa. All kind of ended up in Chicago. My father was a tool and die maker. They bought an old movie theater not far from here and converted it into a machine shop. My brothers still work in it.

When I got out of high school I worked and then I got married. Now I'm working as admitting clerk in a hospital and I'm also going to college part-time. I might go into medical technology.

ABOUT THE CHILDREN:
I want them to do something that they enjoy doing, not something that they're going to make a million dollars on. These days unless you're somebody very important, you're not going to get rich anyway. So for a few more or less dollars a week you should be doing something that you enjoy doing. If someone would prefer to be a truck driver and really enjoy it because he would see the country or whatever, then I would want him to do that instead of trying to push him for college education.

THREE WISHES:
I would like to have the money to make this house structurally sound. The house is probably the thing I revolve around the most. I don't want to leave it, but it seems like it's just kind of falling apart. And I wish I never had to do the housework. Now that's a practical wish. And I would probably wish for the dog to come back.

ABOUT THE PHOTOGRAPH:
I'd say this photo is more like the family just because of the dog and the books, our two major interests. By the way, the dog ran away when we were on vacation and the children miss her. Each of the children seems to be themselves. Gian is a little defiant and she shows it. She's not going to smile, but she'll look you straight in the face. And Naoma's very natural in the photo. She's always laying down on the floor with the dog. Oh, and Cari likes to joke and I think that comes out there.

DOROTHEA AND ROBERT SEALS

MR. SEALS: Editor on a daily newspaper

Mr. Seals: I was only twenty-five when I hit Chicago. I had been working for a newspaper in Knoxville, Tennessee. Actually, I was on my way to the West Coast and I stopped here and I stayed too long and I ran out of money. So I got a job working for *Billboard* magazine and stayed on. From there I went back into the newspaper business, and I've been here ever since, moving from one newspaper to another. I've been at the *Tribune* now for twenty-five years.

Mrs. Seals: One of the first things that impressed me about Bob was he is one of the few fortunate men in the world. He is doing exactly what he wants to do.

Mr. Seals: I have always liked Chicago. I don't like it as well right now as I used to when I was younger. My life-style has changed quite a bit in the last ten years. Well, I don't hang out in saloons all the time any more. And I'm outdoors quite a bit. I ride a bicycle, run with the dog, go up in the park where the casting pier is.

Mrs. Seals: And we like to follow police calls.

Mr. Seals: Yes, we love to chase cops and chase fires. I have a police radio. At night when we take the dog to the park, if we hear something exciting on we'll take off in a cloud of dust and sometimes get there about the same time as the cops!

Mrs. Seals: I came to Chicago in 1946 having worked in public relations and advertising. I made up my mind I was going to get into TV, and I did become one of the early producers of TV commercials in Chicago. It was the most fascinating period of all my advertising life. But it was hard work. After Bobby and I were married a few years, we found we were making an awful lot of money between us but we didn't see each other. I worked days and he worked nights. So one day I said, "We have no life together. I'm not going back to that old TV hassle. We don't need the money." So I got a job as a part-time typist in an insurance company, and I kept that job for thirteen years. I just grew

to like the life. And we spent more time together and had some very happy years together. Twenty-five last May.

Question: Can you put yourselves in a class?

Mr. Seals: In America, it's principally based on income and, to a lesser degree, education. And according to those standards, I think we consider ourselves, I would say, middle-class to upper-middle-class.

Mrs. Seals: I feel fully accepting of the fact that we're average, middle-class Americans—I mean, in our political, educational, and cultural aspects.

Mr. Seals: I think we're slightly above average, by God. And we are somewhat unconventional compared to the average middle-class family.

Mrs. Seals: Yes, we have a real cross-section of friendships. Friends that range from winos to multimillionaires.

Question: How do you feel about being in a book?

Mr. Seals: I feel interested in that you would be interested in us, but I am not overly impressed with having been chosen to be part of the book. Both of us have certainly been in public life. I certainly have as a reporter and editor. I have had many bylines and pictures published.

Mrs. Seals: That may be the answer for me, too. I've had stories written about me in trade papers. It's nice, you know. I get a kick out of it and I get extra copies and send them to my friends and that kind of stuff. But there's nothing factual about my life that is outstanding. It's been an average life.

ABOUT THE PHOTOGRAPH:

Mr. Seals: I don't think you can tell by looking at a photo what the person's like, really. Actually, you get a hint of my personality by the sandals I wear. It shows that I'm a little bit unconventional.

Mrs. Seals: I think that's a good picture of Bobby. And for myself, I'd say it's a picture of the way I'd like to appear. Not dressy but tailored. Rather formal, and by formal, I mean restrained, not effusive.

[170   ]

LAURA AND KEN SMITH
CHILDREN: IAN, SCOTT, KELLY, HOLLY

MR. SMITH: Commercial artist

Mr. Smith: I have lived in this area basically for the last dozen years. I really wouldn't want to live anywhere else.

Mrs. Smith: Yes, and really the foremost reason why we live here is because Ken works three blocks from here. He comes home for lunch every day and he's home by four o'clock in the afternoon. I like this neighborhood. I like the convenience. I like not having to own a car.

Mr. Smith: I'm a commercial artist. I'm basically in the layout and design field. I am general manager of a fairly good-sized studio, one of the bigger studios of its kind in the city. I've worked at this particular job about fifteen years and stuck with it because I liked it very much and liked the people I work with. And I've developed myself to the point where to some extent I am one of the people who control the business. I'm a great work-oriented person, although not to the point where—I hope I don't neglect my family.

My father was an immigrant from Scotland. He was the last of eleven children. He went into the army when he was fourteen years old, the First World War. He only had an eighth-grade education. My mother came from Tennessee. She was one of ten children. My father became an accountant with the IRS, actually a field agent. We were poor until my father got fairly well up in the IRS. We didn't have heat in our house until I was about eleven years old, and the only heat we had was a wood-burning stove in the kitchen. But my father eventually did all right. He did all right enough to the point that when I went to high school I was able to go to a private high school. And so did my brother. And my brother got a scholarship at a very good university and became a priest.

Mrs. Smith: I am the second of four girls. My father is an ex-football player. He used to play for Northwestern. And he never had any sons. But he taught his daughters that they did not require a man to support them, that they were all intelligent and perfectly capable of taking care of themselves. And in our household education was foremost. I am a housewife and mother, which is not exactly what my father had intended. I'm the only one of the four so far that has done that. I would say that somebody had to. But my father loves it.

I've had a career—I was in public relations, and I imagine some day I will go back. But for right now I'm perfectly happy. I don't want to go to work.

Question: How do you feel about being in a book?

Mr. Smith: Love it. What the hell.

Mrs. Smith: With forty-two workmen walking in and out of this house every day, I live publicly. We have nothing to hide, and we're about as straight as two people can be.

ABOUT THE PHOTOGRAPHS:

Mr. Smith: The indoor shot shows us in our current state of disarray. We're building a house, and everything is totally up for grabs. A total mess. And we're smiling through it.

Mrs. Smith: The indoor picture says it. But I could never show it to my mother. She doesn't see how we can live here, let alone allow ourselves to be photographed in it.

Mr. Smith: The outside shot looks a bit like a painting. And I like these two feet sticking up there.

MEG AND DAVID BARR

CHILD: DAVID-JASON
CAT: CALICO

MRS. BARR: Library worker
MR. BARR: Unemployed

Mr. Barr: Where I was raised was essentially a steel town near Baltimore. My father was probably the last person to become a metallurgist without a college degree. I don't think he finished high school. And like he started out working in the mills, in the blast furnace, like anybody else at that time. And just worked straight through. When I was twelve my parents got divorced. I got real involved with, kind of into a religious trip at the time. Probably to compensate. I joined the Church of the Brethren.

When I was eighteen I went to college in Bridgewater, Virginia. It's a small Church of the Brethren–related school. And after college I went into a seminary. I was studying for the ministry for three years. And then, let's see. I was in Mississippi one summer with the civil rights thing. And the next summer I had a church of my own for three months. It was actually a place where they had lay ministry so I didn't need to be ordained, down in southern Missouri about forty miles from a paved highway. At the same time, well, I was getting real into a social-consciousness kind of thing at the time. And I decided to become a caseworker in the city. And later I got a job as a union steward for the public aid office.

You're wondering what all this has led to? That's what I'm trying to find out. I currently have a lot of interests, you know, in a lot of things. I'm just trying to find out what I can fit into right now. I think what I'm going to try next, just in terms of survival, is applying for jobs at hospitals doing the interviewing that refers people to public aid. You know, it's the same work really. It's just from the other side. My ideal make-believe job would be writing— freelance writing in a kind of area where I could have a couple of specialties and switch off.

Mrs. Barr: My father's parents were both off the boat from Ireland. And my mother's mother was Canadian. My father is one of those people who loves to work, eighteen hours a day. He's a photographer and works for a Catholic publication. He's always in his darkroom, working all the time. My mother worked full-time until the day she died. She was a dietitian over at the Veterans Hospital. But every time we would come home from school, she would have time for whatever we wanted. My mother made her own decisions, but she always pretended that my father had the final say and that she was a meek little housewife. I don't think that one should ever pretend that they have to rely on the wishes of another person like that. They should be independent.

Question: Do you have any hopes or ambitions for your child?

Mrs. Barr: I kind of wouldn't like him to be a President or a political idiot, and I don't think he's that stupid. And I really would not like to see him become some professional cruncher or beater-upper, you know, like a soldier or a football player. Other than that, I don't care.

I do have hopes for myself. I'd like to be a midwife or something like that. If I can handle stillbirths and miscarriages I would really want to go to school and get my R.N. and become a midwife. If I can't cope with them, I'll do pediatrics. Right now I work in a library. I'm getting to the point where I can't handle the hours or the pay. You see, I'm doing all the work at the library that a person who has gotten their master's degree would do, only I don't get paid for it because I don't have the degree.

ABOUT THE PHOTOGRAPH:

Mrs. Barr: It looks like the way I feel about David and D.J. Very happy and comfortable. You know, blue jean–type thing. We're an informal family. We enjoy each other. We don't impose a whole lot of rules on each other or on D.J. Very relaxed, and it's not a whole bunch of manners.

MARY PITTMAN
CHILDREN: CARL, JANIE, JEANIE

MS. PITTMAN: Nursery school assistant and part-time college student

Well, I was born in Chicago. I stayed on the West Side most of my life until about five years ago when I moved to the North Side. Oh wow, the North Side, it's better. It's better because on the West Side it mostly was blacks, and the people was nice but it's just if you get hurt, it wasn't too great. The policemen really didn't have time or whatever. They more or less didn't care. But here you stand a better chance. Because if someone tried to break into your home here, the policemen usually be here quick, you know. Maybe if I call them it would take them like fifteen minutes to get here. And then again if I called them on the West Side it may take forever, you know.

My grandmother raised me. And she raised the four of us, which was two sisters and one brother. My mother and father—they like left us, you know. And my grandmother hated to send us to an orphanage. So she kept us because she wanted us to be together as sisters and brother. She was my father's mother.

She was a hard-working lady—working at the hospital trying to support four children on her own. Many a time we had to get charity from the Catholic Church and live off that. But it was a very nice warm home. She gave us the love. We didn't have the money but she did give us the love. She sent all three of my brothers and sisters through high school, herself. And they had to have gym shoes, lunch money, and she would strive to get them through high school.

With my children I'm trying to do the same things—give them plenty of love. A lot of people misunderstand the money and material things and they give them everything they want, and they still don't have the love. And then the children, nine out of ten times, turn out to be no good.

I'm having a little problem with my son because I am trying to raise him too. And it's not fair with all the women around now and not a man. It's hard for him and he more or less fights out. You know, "Leave me alone."

I will tell them the importance of going to school, to get a better education. But more or less, I just refuse to force them to go. And I just hope that maybe one day—if we all live that long—that life will go better for them than it has for me.

I work at the Mary Crane Nursery since last September. I'm more or less like a teacher assistant. I'm going to school to be a student teacher, at National College of Education, and I have a year and a half to finish up. I've been going part-time for four years now.

THREE WISHES:
I would wish for a father for my children. I would wish for understanding toward everyone in this world, and I would also wish for a home. Yes, a home, not an apartment, where my kids can enjoy themselves.

Question: How do you feel about being in a book?
I like the idea. I really feel flattered to even be thought about.

ABOUT THE PHOTOGRAPH:
It's all together. The flowers are showing and it just looks like a beautiful home. It looks like a person who is trying to better herself. That's the way I look. Well, trying to reach my goal in life. A working mother and going to school part-time trying to be a sole support. I love it. I really do. At first I started to call you back and say to you I couldn't do it. Because I thought you had to be real dressed. And then I called Terry and she told me, "No, just wear what you have." So I just put on that. This is a family photo of just completely us. This is art.

SUZANNE AND RICHARD LUHMAN
CHILDREN: JOHN, PHILIP

MR. LUHMAN: Lawyer

Mrs. Luhman: I really expected that once I moved to Chicago that, God help me, I would not wind up in Wilmette [high-income Chicago suburb], but that we would probably have a home in the inner-city area somewhere. And I probably figured that I would die in Chicago, that this would be my last place of residence—because my husband really has the kind of commitments that spell out forever and ever. So when he came home and said, "It's all up for grabs," I was just really flabbergasted and I was extremely excited, very positively excited.

Mr. Luhman: What she is speaking about is that we're contemplating leaving Chicago and going to another locale. We've got an opportunity now that I've sold my practice, to make a move. Personally it's something that I've considered before but never thought I had the financial wherewithal to pull it off with some comfort and some assurance of having a little bit of a cushion in case things don't go right. So we're definitely heading west towards the mountains. And we're leaving pretty darn soon.

Mrs. Luhman: We're going to start our search in two weeks. We're thinking of Idaho, Montana, Colorado. We are looking for a place with a climate and environment that is more conducive to enjoying life, where we can be outdoors as much as possible.

Mr. Luhman: I feel I need a complete break from this community and this mode of practice. I've currently been engaged in practicing law in my own firm in essence, and it involves maybe twelve, thirteen hours a day, and I'm working six days a week. And I don't want to practice on that basis. I would be willing to get involved again in private practice with a lesser commitment in terms of the hours I have to put in. Obviously I'll cut my standard of living. But I'm prepared to do that. I think there are more important things than marrying a job. I've married a wife and some children and a collie and a whole bunch of fish and tadpoles and that's where I'm going. And that's really where it counts, particularly the lady.

Mrs. Luhman: I find the large city to be exciting, and for me personally I don't mind, but it's a hellish place to raise a family. When my kids go out on the street to play, I'm generally pretty glad to see them come home in one piece. I really don't fear so much from the adult population as I do older kids that are in their teens who are bored and mischievous and just looking for something to pass the time of day.

Question: Can you put yourselves in a class?

Mrs. Luhman: How about *independent*? You know, a year and a half ago I could have said *divorced* and that would have given me a class. But I am not any longer. And since I have been married and out of the mountains and into the city all at once, I've had an identity crisis. I really don't know. If I were to go into a shop to buy some clothing that would befit a woman of my station I don't know whether I would buy jeans or a damn sable stole. I have never really identified myself with a class. Mentally I think I am a working-class person because when I am working I am happier. And all of the work that I have ever done that I have enjoyed has been in a line of service, whether it be working in a hospital or cutting men's hair, which was my most recent work.

Question: How do you feel about being in a book?

Mrs. Luhman: I think we found it exciting. We've just been married a year, and it's given us a chance to look at ourselves from a perspective that we wouldn't have been looking at before. It has given us some insight. And you've made me think. I like that.

ABOUT THE PHOTOGRAPH:

Mrs. Luhman: I think that photograph definitely looks and feels like us. It's very hard to say what other people would see in it.

MARY AND WILLIAM HARRINGTON

MRS. HARRINGTON: Cashier
MR. HARRINGTON: Policeman

Mr. Harrington: I'm a community relations officer. Well, our job is trying to help out people that are on their uppers. You know, destitute. I like being able to help people.

This job became official in 1967, but in 1962 I went over to the housing project and started the same type of work there on my own. Now I work the entire district, helping the needy out when they get in a jam. Not legal jams—I'm no lawyer, don't pretend to be—but when they need advice on what to do for one thing or another, no jobs, no food, no clothing, being dispossessed of their homes, something like that.

My job is better than being a patrol officer. I find it more interesting than going out and grabbing hoods and putting them away. Like now I try to get these youngsters before they go bad and try to straighten them out, try to get them to abide by the things that are proper.

I was an MP during the war. I had five and a half years in the military service. When I came back from the war I made an application to the Chicago police department. So I've been a policeman for almost thirty years.

As far as I'm concerned, there's nothing like Chicago. I grew up here. My father was a poultry salesman on the South Water Street Market. I think that Chicago is far superior to any city that I've ever known. A guy can always find a job in Chicago and make a buck if he wants to. I grew up during the Depression and I was able to find a job then, and I was only a kid. I even like the climate in Chicago.

I think that Richard Daley is one of the finest mayors in the entire world. And he's out to make Chicago a better place to live and work. And I think he puts in twenty-three hours and thirty minutes a day trying to make this a better city.

Mrs. Harrington: My parents were Irish. They were about eighteen when they came over. I grew up in Chicago on the Northwest Side. My father was a motorman on the streetcars. But he died very young. I met my husband during my last year of high school.

I'm a cashier at a clothing store. Oh, I enjoy it. Meeting people all day long. When my kids were in school I went out and got a job and I've been working ever since.

ABOUT THE PHOTOGRAPHS:

Mr. Harrington: It's O.K. to use either photo, but I don't like the way my feet are in A. And I'm winking in B. In B there are the photographs of my daughters and awards that I received in the police department. The only thing is I don't have any of my guns or my fishing tackle up there. It would give a better idea of what sports the wife and I follow.

Question: Is the photograph at all misleading?

Mr. Harrington: The only thing is that you wanted me in uniform. I usually work in civilian clothes.

ABOUT THE AUTHOR

Born and raised in Chicago and currently a resident of the city, Roslyn Banish studied photography at the Institute of Design of the Illinois Institute of Technology. She received a M.S. degree in photography in 1968 under Aaron Siskind, and also had Arthur Siegel as a teacher. She then taught photography at Harrow College in England and in 1973 was awarded a grant by the Arts Council of Great Britain to photograph London families. Her work has been exhibited in the United States and England.